I0067324

Women EMPOWERMENT at Work:
Create Your Own Success

LISA TIERNEY, CSLC

Copyright © 2015 Lisa Tierney

All rights reserved. No part of this publication may be reproduced or transmitted in any form or by any means, without permission from the author or Publisher. Reviewers may quote brief passages.

ISBN: 978-1-63103-016-1

Published by CaryPress
www.CaryPress.com

TESTIMONIALS

In *Women Empowerment at Work: Create Your Own Success*, Lisa Tierney provides a truly useful book that every working woman should read. As I read the book, I couldn't help but think, "My sister, niece, friend needs to read this." *Women Empowerment at Work: Create Your Own Success*, offers the reader practical advice and how to steps that every working women can relate to regardless of the profession or title.

Tierney writes in an easy-to-follow style injected with light hearted humor which makes *Women Empowerment at Work: Create Your Own Success* an enjoyable read as useful. You definitely will be employing Tierney's tips for years to come. If you care about mentoring women, you should get them *Women Empowerment at Work: Create Your Own Success*.

Sharen Nocella
Chief Marketing Officer
Obermayer Rebmann Maxwell & Hippel LLP

***

I found *Women Empowerment at Work: Create Your Own Success* to be incredibly insightful! I enjoyed reading about the successful women from all walks of life and their journey towards empowerment.

The author's touch upon a myriad of discerning points was done exceptionally well. Demonstrating how to implement suggestions through illustrations of scenarios and replies/responses was definitely impactful. I applaud the author for being a successful woman who has achieved a keen level of discernment. I greatly appreciate the fact that she has a love for humanity and responsibility to try to make this world a better place. A book that shares women's secrets of empowerment is certainly a rarity in the corporate setting - especially among females for various reasons.

Melissa Presbery, ARM
Philadelphia Insurance Companies
A Member of the Tokio Marine Group

***

"Lisa provides very practical recommendations for professional women to help them manage their time, balance their lives and overcome some of the challenges they face along their journeys toward becoming "rising stars" at their organizations. As I read her experiences and the experiences of some of her clients, I found myself nodding my head in agreement with the recommendations she candidly, wittingly and meaningfully shares in each chapter of this book."

Blythe Seese,
Director of Business Development
Kreischer Miller Elko & Associates

***

I followed Lisa Tierney's process for identifying what you want that is covered in the first chapter of her book *"Women Empowerment at Work: Create Your Own Success"* I chose more revenue as my primary want. Two days later, I find out that a colleague of mine referred me for a large, lucrative project! Maybe that was coincidence, but maybe it was because I declared what I wanted. Read this book to gain greater empowerment and achieve your goals.

Judy Weintraub,
CEO SkillBites LLC

***

This is a great and beneficial read! It immediately caught my interest and kept it going right until the end. The author writes as if she is speaking to you in conversation, causing the words to lift right off the pages. I was inspired and motivated by the experiences, accomplishments, and lessons learned from the author and other women who shared their stories in this book. I could realistically imagine myself in the situations and applying the author's recommendations to my business and workplace. The content is very relevant and incorporates the happenings in today's fast-paced, modern world. The teachings in this book helped me to take my career to the next level. After many years as a manager, group exercise instructor, trainer and certification specialist in the fitness industry, I wanted to start filming and sharing my own professional fitness videos but was stumped as to how to go about it. I incorporated many of the tips in this book, starting with knowing what I wanted and asking for it. I am now making those fitness videos!

If you want to be an empowered woman at work, this is a must-read. Even if you are an empowered woman already, you'll find yourself nodding your head in agreement and it will only strengthen and reaffirm what you already know. It gives realistic and easy to follow tips to be a better you. For males, this book is beneficial, too, as it offers insight into a woman's perspective in the workplace as well as the different and similar concerns we share. There is advice in this book that can be followed on a daily basis and it is a great reference when setting big goals at work.

Michelle Olowolafe,
Fitness Instructor

***

This book really helped me to enhance my relationships at work and more effectively address the issues that concern me. I became more proactive in dealing with situations I was trying to avoid before. I recommend this book to any woman that needs help in resolving some difficult situations in the office.

Inessa Zolot

***

Lisa Tierney hit a home run with her book *Women Empowerment at Work: Create Your Own Success.* Beginning with understanding a woman's natural thought process, tendencies, including stories from real women in diverse businesses, to specific instructions on how to get where you want to be in business, Lisa lays out a path for all women. This book is a great combination of issues and concerns we have all experienced paired with solid coaching on how to address these issues. Read it yourself and give it as a gift to every woman you know in business!

Lisa Benson

Lisa Tierney

ACKNOWLEDGEMENTS

I want to give special thanks to the wonderful female community who volunteered to share their secrets with the readers of my book. Some of these ladies are old friends and trusted colleagues and some brought special new gifts of friendship and sharing to me with their short stories that revealed their personal stories of accomplishment. They are especially empowered and spirited women – the kind we should all seek out – professionally as well as personally. These empowered women are:

Paula Green	(Know What They Want)
Petra Diener	(Harness the Essence of Their Passion)
Gabrielle Luoma	(Motivate Others)
Dana Spain	(Act Confident)
Sherry Ziesenheim	(Speak Impeccably)
Dena Lefkowitz	(Manage Their Time)
Joy Taylor	(Embrace Others)
Jill Lock	(Respect Themselves)
Kathy Sautters	(Demonstrate Your Value)
Patricia Dinkens	(Stay Educated)
Teri A.	(Improve their Environment)
Rebeca Watkins	(Acknowledge Family Dynamics)
Michelle Lifschitz	(Share Their Secrets)

And to all the thoughtful, caring and generous women who took the time to encourage me to write the book, to read my final draft, provide reviews and make meaningful recommendations for improvements to the book, you are too many to mention here but you know who you are.

DEDICATION

To my mother, who taught me first-hand about the possibilities for reinventing yourself. She went from being an administrative assistant to an Admiral at the navy base, in Bayonne, New Jersey, where she met my dad, to a position with the Hudson County Sheriff's office, rising through the ranks to become one of the first female Captains. Along the way, she also received her college degree by attending night school and continued on to get her Masters in Education. She even managed to get student teach for six months, commuting to New York. She did all this while raising my brother and me through elementary and high school, eventually caring for my father through a terminal illness. I have to say, looking back I can't imagine how she did it all (including switching all of our clothes out each season from the closets in the attic to taking all the air conditioner units out of the windows each fall. She took care of all of the shopping and spent a lot of time with me. In my opinion, she never skipped a beat.

In truth, she often complained about her in ability to stay home and "just raise my kids" and approached her career with a good bit of resentment (as you can imagine, it would not have been easy for her in such a male-dominated world – especially since she was a strong, intelligent and attractive woman). But the woman I saw capably juggled it all and inspired me to choose to have both a career and motherhood. As she served as my inspiration, it is my hope that I will live my life in such a way that proves to my daughter that she can be anybody she wants to be – and that I will love and support her always – no matter what.

CONTENTS

EMPOWERED WOMEN AT WORK …

PREFACE

Why are so many women disillusioned and disengaged at work?

As a life coach for female professional service providers, I can assure you that I hear the same complaints each and every day from my female clients who feel beaten down by their supervisors and counterparts. As a professional woman, having worked in a corporate environment for nearly 20 years, I relate to their feelings of inadequacy and lack of control. Truth is, this is not just a woman's problem. Disenchantment among corporate America (and the rest of the world) has become very common among many individuals who feel caught up in a "rat race" and feel there is no way out. Current developments such as increased mergers of companies due to a diminishing workforce of retiring Baby Boomers and an ever-changing global landscape are making professional environments even more problematic.

Recently, my daughter asked me if I won the lottery and was able to receive $10,000 each week would I still work?" I replied with a smile and said, "Sure!"

Throughout my life, I have always been a keen observer. I have witnessed my life as much as lived it, always attracted to figuring out why people did this or why someone would say that. Always a truth-seeker, I asked many questions, read numerous texts and have come to learn a lot. I have applied these lessons to my professional life with fantastic results. For years now, I have enjoyed an incredibly rewarding professional experience. I am my own boss, leading myself toward a future that serves me, my family, and humanity with the best of intentions. I am calm, secure and confident about the value I provide, the fees I charge and the results that occur. I feel empowered each and every day and am no longer criticized or undervalued. I haven't had a confrontation in years. Life for me is truly a dream come true. Work is no longer work – it is a joy. I have been honored to share many of my lessons learned about how to thrive in the corporate world with my female coaching clients and have rejoiced as they have achieved their own successes. I decided that it was time to share these insights with more women than I can touch in my individual client practice. I expect that the information provided to you on the following pages will help you to achieve the same success in your professional life so that you can feel fulfilled, rewarded and valued at work. If you are a professional woman or are a young woman who plans to enter the workforce someday, you should receive great benefit from reading this book.

I will be completely honest with you throughout this book, using real life examples as I share what I have learned throughout the years (using different names, of course). I also have the honor of sharing some stories from other empowered professional women who learned some of these same lessons along the way.

YOU, Too, Can Be EMPOWERED at Work…!

OK, women listen up. It is time! It's time for women to rise up, take charge and change some things. Look around. Unstable global politics. Alarming environmental issues for our planet. A fragile international economy. Religious persecution. Poverty. Ignorance. Fear. War. We see inequality and injustice every day – all the time. And we care. We care but we don't DO enough. Historically, we have left far too much of the fixing to men. And that has possibly made sense so far … to understand why the world is the way it is today is to understand one of the most important distinctions between men and women. It's our brains. Simply put, we are wired differently. Men's brains are wired to take action and women's brains are wired to take care. There are many fascinating studies on how our brains work differently and I encourage you to do some more Internet research and educate yourself and your children. In fact, I wished I had known more about these differences when I was younger. Having gone to an all-girl high school, I missed out on some important lessons in how differently boys process information.

Men have tendencies to process information more linearly and take action for immediate change whereas women process information more holistically, considering more of the ramifications around a particular action taken. This simple fact about women's brains implies that women are more efficient at managing groups because they are better equipped at considering all involved. It means that women are better wired to multitask. Surprised? Women take into account everything and all involved when making any decision. It might make us seem a bit less decisive to our male counterparts but that's because we are taking much into consideration.

I was speaking to a male president of a company about how, all of a sudden it seemed, he found himself in charge of a lot more women at his organization. He was very forthcoming and admitted to me that he found females to be better at handling the company's clients because, he said "They're really so much better at managing relationships. They listen to the clients and they ask great questions. The only thing is they're so *emotional*, ya know?" So, a lesson can be learned here. Men don't relate to the emotional. Just take a note. Don't take it as a criticism. Don't take it personally.

Later in this book we will be deeply exploring the role of emotion in the workplace. You might ask yourself at this point, "*Is* being emotional really such a bad thing?" Or you might think, "Well, I certainly agree that being emotional has no place in the office!" This will be a good debate. So keep thinking. And keep reading.

Think back to the first time someone (most likely a man, I would guess) decided that it would be a good idea to take the town's garbage out into a barge to be released out at sea, somewhere in the middle of the ocean. This was a linear decision about what to do with the town's garbage. A woman might have thought about the ramifications of such an action, considering tides, the effects on sea life and possibilities around barges breaking and garbage reaching the shore, etc. (On a personal note, I was once at a beach where we all found ourselves collecting garbage as we waded into the sea, because of a just such an incident.) This is a story I sometimes tell to illustrate my point – and incite women – to realize that it's our obligation, our duty, to speak up and get involved. I can't help but think the world would be a much better and safer place if it were run with a collaborative approach between men and women. I'm not man-bashing here, honestly - because the two brains, working together, perfectly complement each other, each with their individual strengths, enabling both sexes to live together and thrive in this world.

The world has undergone some magnificent changes in the last 50 years. The leaps made by using technology will continue to impact the world in ways that we can't yet imagine. The Internet was originally formed by a small group of scientists who came together to share their information about their individual discoveries for the good of the whole. This has been a consistent theme with technology, as open forums call people together to share their information for the greater good, pressing the fast-forward button of learning through sharing. Think about how the younger generations have a completely different approach to problem-solving. The other day I walked into a Best Buy store (a large retailer of computer products and appliances) and asked a question to a young man wearing a blue shirt, who worked there. He didn't answer me, but rather tapped for a bit on his hand-held tablet and waited. He was acquiring a forum to research my question. He then started talking into his ear piece and a few other staffers responded to him. Eventually, he walked me over to a row of gadgets and presented me with the cable that I needed.

This young man's behavior represents a group approach to problem-solving. It can be a different experience for some – as they may perceive the employee's behavior to have been rudely impersonal; another perspective might deem the young man to be surprisingly efficient. To me, his behavior simply represents a different way of doing things.

Speaking of shopping in stores, cashiers can't complete a sale unless they go through a series of prompts that come up in their computers. For example, when checking out at Toys R Us, you are asked if you will need batteries and at McDonald's, you are asked, "Do you want fries with that?"

This is a way that, using technology, we can process and enforce the use of successful strategies for conducting business, problem solving and getting answers. The design behind this is a holistic one, taking all kinds of various scenarios into consideration in order to find proof an outcome.

This is how women's brains work naturally.

Now seems the perfect time for women to rise up into more leadership roles. Because, as the world becomes a smaller place, languages, geography, time zones, race and gender become less separating factors and women around the world are receiving higher, equal levels of education. In the Western world more men are sharing the duties of caring for younger and elder family members. Everything is in place to level the fields around anything that used to keep women out of the workplace – and out of important positions of power and influence that significantly affect our world.

I firmly believe that there is room for improvement in how women stand up for themselves and support each other - at home and in the workplace.

If you feel powerless to change anything at work, if you feel like there's no way you can lead others, or take on any more responsibility than you already have, I beg you to keep reading. I assure you that each chapter will educate, enlighten and inspire. And I will offer specific action items for you to consider and *do* during your next business day. Because, along the way of assuming more *power* – which I am asking you to do – you will also find something else ... you will find gratification at work. You will find your voice, discover in yourself strengths you never knew you had, and you will enable others to achieve more than they could have imagined. You will come to enjoy the benefits of a much more enjoyable professional experience.

You, too, can be EMPOWERED at work!

1 - Empowered Women At Work...Know What They Want

During my first interview at my sales company, an HR rep proudly told me that the company almost always hired and promoted from within. Then she told me that I was overqualified for the position and that I'd be bored quickly and that's why she decided not to hire me. Since I had nothing to lose, I countered with "Well, if you promote from within and I'm as overqualified as you say, I shouldn't have this job long enough to get bored." I got the job.

For years, I was able to successfully work my way "up the ranks." But after some time, I found myself completely stalled. It was my longest term position there and I'd learned a lot, but I felt it was now time to move on. Easier said than done.

I had my heart set on a sales job that I knew I could do, and do well. However, I was told by many that these positions were reserved for people with sales experience and contacts. I had neither, but that didn't stop me from applying for every sales job that opened – four in four years. Each time the hiring manager refused to interview me, due to my lack of experience and qualifications. "No, No, No, NO." Those were a lot of no's – even for an experienced no getter such as I.

When I applied for the 5th posting, the head of HR called me into his office and asked me why I kept applying for a job that I was "clearly not going to get."

I proceeded to tell him all the things I would have told the sales manager, had she agreed to interview me, including the deep experience I had with our products, which I learned over the years, having worked my way up through the ranks. I pointed out how my particular experience would serve our customers more effectively and that my skills offered much more than other salespeople with general contacts and sales experience.

The sales manager was asked to interview me and I got that sales job.

In fact, not only did I get that job, but nine months later, I was promoted to a national sales position that was so specialized, it was the only one of its kind in the company. At the end of my first year in that position, I won Salesperson of the Year (out of 500 sales people). Over my 30 year sales career, many other awards followed.

- Paula Green – Director National Sales, Credit Marketing Services, FactorTrust, Inc.

Let me tell you how I developed the credo that I use to live my life. It was a line delivered in a silly romantic comedy starring Reese Witherspoon. It was a lousy movie in which she played a shallow woman. I don't think I even chuckled once while watching it. But I was so grateful for watching this movie because of the wonderful lesson it taught me. There was a scene where her character briefly considers seeing a therapist but changes her mind. She peeks her head back in the office to ask, "In general, from all the clients you see and all that you've learned, is there just one thing you can tell me that will help?" And that's when the therapist delivers the line, "Figure out what you want, then learn how to ask for it."

Note: My male editor commented here, that "A man would say, 'Figure out what you want, then go get it!' "

Up until that point, my credo had been just the first part. I used to say, "Figuring out what you want is the hard part – getting what you want is easy." I had forgotten about the asking. I have since embellished another part of the credo. Sometimes it's a matter of stating what you want out loud. Just *telling* people what you want. The more you tell, the better, in fact.

I now tweak the credo as it will best serve whoever I'm speaking to. So, let's review: knowing exactly what you want is a critical first step. Next comes what you do with that information.   Ask someone to help you get it? Tell someone this is what you want – tell everyone this is what you want? Yes, you're on the right track. Let's start with the first part – figuring out what you want.

This is where I'm going to ask you to have an out-of-body experience - dozens of times a day, in fact. Before you walk into the meeting, before you step into the office, before you pick up the phone, before you hit that "SEND" button, do you know what you want…exactly what you want to come out of the interaction or exchange? Have you made it perfectly clear in your mind, on your tongue, in that e-mail? If not, then stop right there!

How many times do you walk into a meeting - perhaps it's a weekly department or service area meeting at your place of employment - just because this is what you do every Monday. How many meetings have you been invited to – individual meetings or groups – and you accept the meeting invite on your calendar without having any idea what is to be done at this meeting or why it's been called? How many lunch invitations have you accepted without having a well-formed outcome of why you're about to spend ninety minutes out of the office with this person?

I believe that most of us are on auto-pilot at work. Just saying yes, and hitting buttons and moving throughout the day without knowing WHY we are doing most of it.   My advice to women is to stop and contemplate more of what it is we want from every interaction and exchange that we are having at work.   This includes realizing, for yourself, that you are about to walk into Jane's office this morning to idly chit-chat about the weekend or to badmouth a co-worker – or to share your exasperation in dealing with your teenager at home, etc. Just know that's what you want before you walk in there.   And by knowing what you really want before you do it, perhaps you will still do it, perhaps you will not - perhaps you will do it somewhat differently. By the way, contemplation of well-formed outcomes of your actions can also address the severe issues of mismanaged time, which is another thing I frequently hear about from females in the workplace. "I need to manage my time better." I hear this constantly and we will discuss this more in a bit.

In addition to knowing what you want, you also need to realize a little more of what you don't want. And this is an important step in taking control of your overall professional experience. If you know what you want, then you are more likely to focus on that. Of course, there has to be clarity around the goal and an emotional commitment as to why you seek this goal. Maintaining your focus on the "brass ring" should keep you on track. This way, you are less likely to go and chew the fat with "Jane" – and are more likely to excuse yourself from Jane if/when she is taking your time and energy away from your well-formed outcome by either inviting you into her office or walking into yours to focus on something that will deter you from the goal at hand – getting what you want at work.

I'm not saying that you have to stop camaraderie all together at work – we should enjoy a little "down time" with our colleagues. We should all enjoy friendly interaction with our clients, too and other vendors with whom we interact on a regular basis. I work with many professional women, mostly professional service providers – CPAs, attorneys, financial planners, insurance brokers, etc. - whose intellectual property is their product. Relationships are the key to their success – and understanding how they can effectively manage their key relationships can greatly fuel their career.

Nurturing key relationships is how we human beings achieve success here on Planet Earth, generally speaking. Think about it. Money in and of itself doesn't bring happiness; it buys you things. Other people can, however, positively impact your experience.

When you identify the right group of people that can offer you the essence of what it is you want (i.e. new clients, access to a vacation house or an elite summer camp for your kids) then those are the people that you should spend time with.

I once heard a basketball player speak at a conference. He shared something he had heard that would predict how much money you would make each year. He said that if you averaged the annual income of your four closest friends, the result would represent your own salary. Wow. That statement alone should get you thinking about who you are hanging out with – at work, at school – and what about the friends your kids are making? Interesting....Is he right?

Establishing, and nurturing, rapport with *the right group of people* can truly enhance your professional experience. It's important to realize the need to nurture the right "network" (group of people) because this can bring you success. An important step in getting what you want will be to know which group of people you will nurture – those who can get you what you want.

Do you know what you want? If you are a professional services provider, think about the ideal client you are trying to attract. If you are a manager or a leader of a team at work, figure out what kind of people you need on your team. If you want to make more money, there are a variety of ways to do this. First ask yourself what you want the money for. Write down a few different scenarios. Think about which makes the most sense for you. Then "feel" it. Picture getting what you want in the long-term. Really embrace the possibilities. Let yourself imagine it – dream big! If it feels really good, you're on the right track.

Now make a list of a few people that you could talk to about how you might apply this scenario to your life.

What is it you want?

This is the time when I will ask you to stop reading this book. Put it down and type, text yourself or get a piece of paper and a pen and write it out.

Here are some of the most common things I have heard from women professionals:

At work, I want…..

To feel appreciated
To make more money
To become partner
To get a corner office
Have more time to myself
To be more respected
To be trusted
To bring in more client revenue
To bring in new clients …

I'm not sure how many "wants" you came up with, but let's pick the one thing that we want most…now. And let's work on one at a time, shall we? Select one goal and say it out loud. Like you mean it. Ask yourself why you want this goal? Write this down! Who are you when you have achieved it? How would you feel if you if had this or completed this goal? How motivated are you to achieve this? Write it down, too. Be clear on all this.

Now that we have something that you want, we can start making it happen.

Now that you have set a clear goal ask yourself when you will know that you have it. How will you know, specifically, that you have achieved this goal? See the examples below for ideas:

To feel appreciated	My boss, Larry, says he appreciates me
To make more money	I make $75k a year
To reach the top at my firm	I am a partner in 3 years

To get my own office	I have a private office in 12 months
Have more time to myself	I enjoy 3 weeks of vacation each year
To be more respected	I enter work feeling completely confident
To be trusted	People confide in me at work
To bring in more revenue	I generate $20k annually in new sales
To bring in new clients	I bring in 5 new XX type of clients

This part is important because we need to set reasonable clear expectations for ourselves. This is a good practice for others, too – for instance, during reviews of underlings or in mentoring. Motivation drives behavior so it's important to know exactly what you want, why you want it, and how you'll know when you have achieved it. Next, we have to identify the first step in seeing this to fruition.

Now I will ask you to list what behaviors or attitudes will have to change in order for you to start this ball rolling. If you want something to change, you're going to have to do something differently, agreed? Hopefully, you are willing to take the first step in what might seem like a daunting or unrealistic process. See more examples of what I mean as follows:

To feel appreciated	I demonstrate my value regularly at work
To make more money	I have a clear plan for me to make $75k
To reach the top at my firm	I am aligned with a sponsor at

	work
To get my own office	Identified criteria for obtaining an office
To have more time to myself	I will arrange 3 weeks of vacation annually
To be more respected	I treat myself and others with respect
To be trusted	I don't gossip about others
To bring in more revenue	I ask my referral sources for introductions
To bring in more clients	I establish/maintain a referral network

The lesson learned is maintaining a heightened state of awareness – at all times – around what you want and who can help you get it. This is critical to your empowered success. Having a well-formed outcome, as well as a strategic plan of how you will go about achieving that outcome, will go a long way.

Now, remember these two tips about getting what you want:

#1. It really helps if you focus on the desired outcome, which should be a positive for more than just you (in other words, others will be positively impacted by this goal / desire – your colleagues, your company and or humanity.

#2. If you are emotionally connected to the goal / desire, it will help you to stay motivated - and continue to perform the action items necessary - to achieve this goal.

2 - Empowered Women At Work...Harness the Essence of Their Passion

For me, staying in one place is painful.

When I was 16, I decided I wanted to work in the performing arts. A couple of years later, I graduated with a Master of Arts in Drama, Literature and Education and was running a theatre, directing and working as a dramaturge. I soon headed into my first "real" permanent job as a talent manager. After only two years, I realized this wasn't for me after all. It wasn't because of the job itself, it was because of its feeling of permanency.

It seemed to me like I was locked into a life-long contract. And so began my life-long struggle with being true to "my own thing" (which changed from time to time) and a resistance "permanency."

I headed out into the great wide world of self-employment, not quite realizing that it might not pay the bills as well as the permanent job. But I was young, full of energy and wasn't afraid of working two or more jobs at the time – as long as I could do "my own thing." It worked and I liked it. Later, I was offered a job in the (at the time) unknown and spooky world of IT (information technology). This job wound up getting the better of me! It wasn't the money - it was the world it offered me. For years I lived out of suitcases and was able to live in different countries. As I was infected with "itchy feet" I changed directions again – going back to drama, movies, and coaching. Eventually, I decided to sell everything, pack and start from scratch again – this time to the U.K – and this time, I was not 25.

I am currently self-employed and starting new – again. And that's the way I like it - my life, my decisions. Am I afraid of how it's going to work out? Why should I be? I'm almost 50 years old. I'm looking back on almost 30 exciting professional years full of priceless experience, amazing friends, living in half a dozen countries, having learned to speak six languages. The current goal is to move with my partner to the

United States, to set up home and business, and spread the spirit of courage.

- Petra Diener, Freelance Writer / Talent & Communications Specialist at 3 Across the Sea / former Marketing Manager, Newfield IT

When you're engaged in an activity you love doing, time melts away. I believe that when you're in "that zone" and you completely lose yourself in whatever you're doing, then that activity is ideal for you. Some might even call it God's work. Others say it might be one of your passions. Is there a way you can harness a little bit of that at work? If you can harness even just a little bit of your passion while attracting what it is you want, then voila! Work, at least while you're able to incorporate that essence of your passion in, is no longer work anymore.

The Story of Sarah

Let me share the story of Sarah with you. She is a female professional service provider I have worked with. Sarah asked to meet with me because she wanted my help in creating a healthcare brochure and also wanted ideas from me how she could contribute to the growth of the healthcare niche of her accounting firm. Sarah was a 50 something year-old professional who was a partner at this regional CPA firm. She worked with five other partners and was an equal shareholder. She had been asked by one of the retiring partners for her help with the transition of his healthcare clients – mostly group medical practices, including several larger cardiology groups. This niche represented a good amount of revenue for the firm and contained some high-dollar – and high-profiled physicians in the area.

Sarah was tough to get a meeting with. The marketing person at the firm had to reschedule our meeting several times and confided in me that Sarah was not too anxious to meet with me at all. When I finally met Sarah, she started to talk about the brochure but I encouraged her to tell me about herself, her passions in life. She eventually divulged some personal information, including the fact that she was married to an older man who would be retiring soon and wanted her to start slowing down her practice. This seemed to be in conflict with the fact that she was being asked to take over a large part of a thriving niche at the firm. Clearly, this would be more work for Sarah and she seemed less than thrilled about the idea.

I asked her who her favorite clients were. She said, hands down, it was auto dealers. Really? I asked her to tell me more. She went on to tell me that her father and two of her brothers all managed or owned auto dealerships while she was growing up. She understood the auto dealer business and respected her family members for their accomplishments in this industry. She had also worked with a couple of auto dealers as clients. As she described her interactions with these clients, sharing some stories, I saw her face light up and she seemed much more relaxed. I asked her, "How do you feel about inheriting all these medical practices?" Sarah let loose and went on to explain that she understood that these were important clients to the firm. These healthcare clients paid the firm and she felt good about the retiring partner asking her to step in for him because it showed he respected her work and she felt pressured to carry on his legacy. But the thought of spending so much time and energy on a type of client that she felt she didn't mesh well with seemed daunting and left her feeling drained – before she even got started. "So, why don't you pursue more auto dealership clients instead?" I asked. "Well, that's what I *should* be doing!" she replied. "Can you help me do that?" So we hatched a plan to have another up-and-coming senior manager be groomed quickly for taking over the medical niche so she could target more auto dealers. She decided, in that moment, to allow someone else to preserve the retiring partner's legacy. She figured out that she could remain committed to helping with that transition in any way she could – albeit from the sidelines. She gave herself permission to succeed on her own terms.

Sarah also told me how much she loved wine, so I suggested we brainstorm on how we could somehow meld her passion into her work life. We decided that Sarah would plan to host a wine tasting event for the auto dealers in the area. All of a sudden, this woman was a marketing maven, calling people personally to attend her event and quickly expanding the network of influencers for her and the firm to woo.

This is how we do it, ladies!

The next story illustrates how one can embrace or harness a personal or knowledge and bring it into "their own at work." This story takes it a step further, because this professional woman was propelled to take action that served the greater good. I define the greater good, also known as the "higher good" to be a goal that serves oneself and also others – such as your employer, others at the office, the local community and/or the whole of humanity. I find that, with women especially, acknowledging the greater good of a goal makes it easier for them to sell the idea – *especially to other women*. The spiritual side of me is pretty sure that more doors open when you are following your goals, harnessing your genuine passions and serving the greater good. I believe that a lot more opportunities seem to present, volunteers show up, money starts coming in, etc. I know that many of you are nodding right now. Think about it. You have seen this in action, too, I'm sure of it!

The Story of Maureen

Maureen worked for a professional services firm where she served not-for-profit organizations. She was not happy, she told me, because there was a bit of a catch to her situation. She was working under another, more senior, professional who had grown this not-for-profit niche under her own name and personal brand. Maureen was also slated to take over for this senior female department head and felt she would be expected to completely manage the niche in seven to ten years. Maureen was not at all excited about this prospect. She didn't speak up at meetings, was very quiet and not very proactive with clients. Her peers sensed that she was generally unmotivated and she received some negative comments during her last performance review. She and I had a conversation, during which I asked her what her passions in life were (she loved running) and why she was serving these not-for-profit organizations. She explained, "I fell into it. They asked me to get involved. One thing led to another and here I am spending a ton of time with this group of people with whom I feel I have nothing in common."

Maureen also told me about a past endeavor in which she had worked with a farming co-op a few years ago. She greatly admired the farmers and the distributors who worked so hard to do something that she respected – they were feeding America. She understood and related to the mindset of these people, whom she respected, admired and felt comfortable with. I encouraged Maureen to start to pay more attention to this group of people and re-visit her old network in the area. She joined her old co-op and started to schmooze at networking events. She got involved in the organization and was soon speaking up at meetings and was completely engaged again. She re-discovered her passion and zest for what she did – at work. It wasn't that long before she started generating new clients from her efforts. She was much more rewarded and became more productive and passionate about her work.

As many professional women realize, there are significant differences between corporate (for-profit) companies and non-profit organizations, just as there are differences between educational/academic organizations and governmental institutions, etc. This is one of the reasons that finding your niche is so important to being happy at work. Because it will usually take somewhere between six months and two years of marketing to a specific target audience before new business starts to come in, working on something that you believe in, that you are genuinely passionate about, will help you "stay in the game." This six month to 12 month timeframe is necessary to fully establish yourself as an expert in your field and grow that all-important referral network.

Two years is a lot of time, so you should enjoy these people, feel confident about what you have to say with them and, maybe most importantly, feel a genuine sense of rapport with them. How do you define rapport? I would say it's a combination of like-mindedness (same age, gender, educational background, etc.) same values / motivations around what is wanted by all sides and a mutual feeling of like, trust, respect and/or admiration. When all this is present, it isn't work anymore. Think about how men have discovered this. They take Fridays off and spend the entire day golfing with friends as opposed to colleagues or clients. They arrange dinners on Saturday night with their clients and their spouses. They arrange to take their clients out to sporting events or concerts. They have figured out how to harness their passions at work. Women should do more of this, too!

Note: At this book's writing, I have just returned from a speaking engagement at a women's leadership conference where this very topic arose. I was surprised at how many women resisted the concept of going out to dinner or socializing, in general, with their clients. Some common obstacles were, "I don't golf and have no intention of learning"; "I would never ask my husband to come with me to a client event or a Saturday evening dinner"; and "I would be very uncomfortable forging a social relationship with a male client."

My comment on this feedback, since it demonstrated strong resistance to bridging the gap between working relationships and social relationships, is that if we are open to finding a way to bridge a gap, truly open to a new approach, a new way of thinking about a situation, then I'm sure we can discover new, innovative ways to do so. I would start by asking colleagues and clients more questions about their personal lives and passions and then look for something to bridge this perceived gap. Suggestions include some general passions that many of us share, such as children, music, food, and art. Be creative! The human race has a lot of commonalities – let's give ourselves permission to unify, I say!

I have many stories like the ones I have shared here – where the professional is completely disengaged at work because they feel they are not understood – because they have not been empowered to embrace their genuine passion and connect it somehow with the work they do. When did we stop asking what people want? Why do we think we can just relegate anybody to work with someone else without stopping to think about personality, culture, age, gender, common interests, etc.? Why don't we talk about what's important to us as it applies to the job we are doing?

Just as a woman carefully considers which friends to invite to the party, then puts thought into the seating arrangements, why wouldn't you give such thought to teams and initiatives at work?

3 - Empowered Women At Work...Motivate Others and Create an Impetus for Change

It was a Tuesday morning and we were holding our weekly staff meeting. The topic of discussion was the implementation of a new software system. A few people were not contributing to the conversation. I took a few steps back. I started asking questions, such as, "Is this something we need to be doing?"

The group consensus was yes. We reminded ourselves why we had committed to this project and started to honestly examine why this project wasn't moving forward. During the conversation, it became evident that two of the team members were not simply on board. One revealed a fear of her capability to customize the software so that it would be effective. Another admitted that she had no interest in the project at all.

I thought to myself, "Well, this is why we have weekly team meetings."

I asked my team "Who is passionate about this and feels best suited to take over this implementation?" And I waited. After about 30 seconds, the last person I ever would have thought would step up to the plate did just that ... I noticed a raised hand and turned to see one of our para professionals. She had come to us about a year and a half ago and we all enjoyed watching her grow and expand her role at our firm. She smiled and said, "OK. I'll do it."

In that moment, I felt so happy for this young woman. She was taking her place in the firm as someone we could really count on. The whole group was positively impacted by her example. I felt like everyone was thinking, "If she can do that, I can do that, too."

I'm happy to report that, in a matter of just one week, this team member was able to fully implement and customize the program, proving this clearly should have been her job all along. By the way, the other team member who admitted that she was not right for the job wound up leaving us – albeit on good terms. (She is in a new position that better suits her talents and needs).

On that special Tuesday morning, we all learned a lesson about motivation. If you can create an environment that supports everyone on the team, no matter what, then people can be honest about their strengths and their vulnerabilities – to the betterment of the entire team.

- Gabrielle Luoma CPA, CGMA
   Chief Executive Officer & Visionary at GMLCPA, PLLC

There are three perspectives from which any person, event or interaction can be experienced: self, other and objective. We are easily caught up in the self-perspective. It is closely protected by ego and gets us into most of our trouble. Achieving the perspective of another helps us to stop arguments among our kids, enables us to know how to write that proposal for the client and why we remember to leave a tip for the maid before we check out of the hotel. We get it. We just don't apply it to conflict and opposition as an accepted rule of engagement - at work.

Effective and empowered female leaders can adopt an objective, un-biased perspective. They understand the points of view from all sides and can make recommendations for the greater good while taking into consideration everyone's personal agenda so they can alleviate personal fears and contribute to the whole in a genuine, comfortable meaningful way.

If I had a dollar for each time I heard one of the following, common objections to getting anything done at work, I would buy a spectacular vacation home! The objections I hear the most often include:

"He just won't do it."

"It will never happen."

"We tried it before but it didn't work."

There is not much an empowered woman can do to change things at work – *alone*.

Empowered professionals – in fact, all successful people - understand how to make people do things differently. It's a very important skill to have. The one thing that we can count on (here on Planet Earth) is change. Time will tick on, people will grow and learn, technology will continue to advance, and in order to compete we must evolve and adapt in ways that will continue to serve our mission and reach our goals.

Although change is constant at work, it always manages to stir discomfort in many professionals.

Change will most likely manifest at your place of business in one of two ways –either you will have to ask your professionals to *stop* doing something or *start* doing something. It can be the adoption of a new software system, welcoming a new employee, merging with another company, or an attempt to uplift low morale or change the culture at your firm. No matter what the goal, you will have to get your people to stop behaving in a manner that might have become routine to them or you will ask them to start doing something new and completely different.

The current consensus where you work might be that there is a long-term behavior (of either doing something wrong or not doing something right) that has been deemed beyond detrimental and simply must change. Yet – nothing happens.

I have heard many sad stories around the perceived inability to change. Some include low-performing employees over whom a group of supervisors spend an agonizing amount of time and energy complaining. Despite numerous hours of conversations, the low caliber employee remains in employment and continues to be tolerated (in many cases, receiving annual bonuses and/or raises, just like his coworkers). Some include the ogre senior manager or the belligerent department head that consistently treats others with harsh criticism and/or explosive outbursts (almost all of us have at least one horror story about someone punching a hole in a wall or screaming at someone in the hall at the top of their lungs at work). Such behavior, although counterproductive and upsetting to many, often goes without any negative consequence. And there are many less dramatic tales of companies consistently losing money to uncollected bills, an ignored crumbling infrastructure or a need for upgraded technology that no one can seem to wrap their arms around at the organization – and so, the problem remains, while employees' morale wanes, money is lost and competitors take control of the marketplace.

Most professionals – especially women – will talk about these necessary changes at work fairly easily in a one-on-one environment. Depending upon whether or not there is careful attention to tone, message and focus (keep the focus of the conversation on the well-formed outcome, please) this will or will not be construed as gossip. Even when most women feel they have successfully swayed each of their counterparts during one-on-one conversations around certain topics, when the time comes for the vote in a group setting at work, or when he or she comes back from the meeting and the woman asks, "Well…what happened?" This same woman is often disheartened to realize that no one stepped up and challenged the issues she fought so hard to for. What happened? Well, one might say this woman chose to allow someone else to do her battle for her.

I want to introduce a new approach for you to use when trying to introduce change at your place of business. Brain science supports the fact that women have a tendency to gain support for their ideas and goals by having individual conversations. Women value connecting with others and so they sometimes travel around the office a few days before the Big Meeting, trying to solidify alliances with certain individuals in hopes that they will bring an important item up for discussion. They will plot to gain other's support through these one-on-one interpersonal exchanges. But there is often great disappointment when either the item never makes it on the agenda, doesn't get discussed, or is quickly shot down with one of the statements I used earlier – such as, "Yeah, that's not a good idea." Idea dropped. Disappointment. Disenchantment. All that wasted time plotting to get our great idea through – what a waste! The new approach I am suggesting you use will be to be brave and make strong, objective, well-intentioned, unemotional and positive power statements at your next Big Meeting. This is a very powerful and effective way to engage everyone. It is foolproof. I want you to try it. I guarantee you will experience some impressive results. It is a game-changer. It is a career-booster. It can also be used to command accountability for employees who are not keeping their promises at work or carrying their own work.

An empowered woman doesn't whine and complain about the way things are. Empowered women know how to get people to do what they want them to do (albeit for the right intentions and the greater good, please). This is the key to your success. The empowered woman gets everyone to rally behind her and offer their strong support around an ideal scenario that she presents. There are tried and true, proven ways to gain support from others around a major initiative or addressing a necessary change at work. The secret is learning how to make an objective, unemotional power statement that addresses everyone's personal agenda. The power statement is then followed with an open-ended thought provocative question that encourages discussion. Hint: Ask the question, then pause...a longer pause is often needed before discussion ensues – be patient. I suggest a six to eight second pause. This may be hard for some women who often feel a need to speak after only four to five seconds of silence in a group environment. If you wait a little bit longer, I think you will be pleasantly surprised by the dialogue that ensues. It's all about the power statement and the question asked.

This a fundamental tool in coaching and a very effective approach to getting people to buy-in to something new. Making a powerful statement about a well-formed outcome addresses an ultimate "What if" scenario …. The delivery of a positive dream delivered in such a way that everyone wakes up and takes notice because they can see themselves as part of the dream. Employees become incited enough to DO something differently because they finally, immediately realize the importance of it, as it applies to them and their personal experience. All of a sudden, there is a shift in attitude or behavior because there is a strong drive to work toward this significant change or improvement. … Wow, how did that just happen? All the great leaders of our time knew how to do this. All the great speeches have these ideal scenarios in them.   So, let's review the winning formula to motivate others and incite change. It starts in a group environment and has three parts:

1.   Power statement that clarifies a well-formed outcome

2.   Question that describes the ideal scenario

3.   Pregnant pause (six to eight seconds)

How do you craft your power statement to be a change agent at work?

A power statement gets everyone's attention and churns up a need for change because it addresses the goals of the whole as it will positively impact each part of the whole (each employee or member of the team). Your power statement should somehow address the personal agendas of those in the room / situation and also inspire everyone. You might not be surprised to learn that everyone would like to ride the wave of success and every employee wants to work for a winning team / company. Success is contagious. A good, thought-provocative question describes an ideal scenario. Allow me to share some examples.

"This company needs to hire five new staff within the next three months in order to meet our client obligations."

"What would it mean to have five employees trained and up to speed by this time next year?"

"We have lost three major clients in the past year, totaling $540,000 in annual revenues."

"What can each of us do, now, to ensure that our remaining clients are satisfied and will be retained?"

"The feedback about John over the last two years has demonstrated poor performance.""

Can we afford not to address this issue?"

Sometimes, you can just go right to the question:

"What would it mean to this organization if we had a customer relationship system that helped us track our pipeline and assisted us with our marketing efforts?"

"What if we could increase our overall revenue by 20% in the next six months?"

"How do you think our employees and customers would react if we supported a local charitable organization?"

These are questions that are designed to get everyone talking about the situation at hand. When there is open discussion, people will offer opinions and, with careful interjections by you, empowered woman, a healthy brainstorming session can take place.

There is another reason that this approach is very effective. If you tell others what to do, without their buy-in, they might actually do it. They might even do it well. But if the group decides this, with each member feeling that they had some control over the situation and participated in devising the solution, and contributed to the agreed-upon actions to be taken, they are far more likely to do engage and do a much better job – as well as have a stronger commitment over the long term.

During your brainstorming session, objections are sure to arise. Limiting beliefs and negative pre-suppositions will manifest themselves. The empowered, brave woman at work should interject and guide the conversation accordingly. Churning up the negative isn't bad; in fact, it's a mandatory part of the change process. But we must be careful to monitor the time and energy spent on the problem. My rule of thumb is no more than 20 minutes before we move away from the problem and toward a proposed solution. These will address those statements that try to shut down the impetus for something new or different. Allow me to share examples of interjections that will keep things on track:

During the discussion about having lost major clients over the past year, it was suggested that everyone stop what they're doing and have a campaign to check in with all the top clients in the firm. Resistance arose:

Objection: *"I don't have time to check in with my clients to see how they're doing."*

Persuasive Question: "How often do you check in with your clients?"

Persuasive Question: "What do you think it would be mean to your client if you were to contact them to simply ask if they are satisfied with our services?"

Persuasive Question: "Would it make sense to use this exercise as means of identifying additional needs of our clients?"

One of the managers in the discussion about the problem employee seemed very resistant that action might be taken that could result in this employee's termination of employment. The empowered woman in the meeting suspected that this was because this employee performed much of the manager's work. The manager might feel that he would have much more work to do himself or have to spend a lot of time training someone else to do the job if the problem employee was terminated.

Objection: *"Alright, I'll have a talk with him – again."*

Power statement: "It seems you are resistant to the firm taking action against John's behavior." (Then wait, not four seconds, more like eight seconds. Let the manager explain himself. He may not even be aware of his feelings)

Persuasive Question: "How much of your client work does John handle?"

Persuasive Question: "Can we help you to delegate some of John's responsibilities to another, more dependable staff member?"

These questions call the manager out, encouraging him to be truthful and open to other more reasonable possibilities. Having yet another conversation with the under-performing employee will surely result in no change. But calling this manager out to honestly assess his objections in a way that safely offers support for this change can address his personal agenda in a supportive way.

How about the need for a new software system that you feel strongly will improve tracking and marketing. You have one or two others in the meeting that simply won't consider it.

Objection: *"We don't have the money right now."*

Persuasive Question: "Are we looking at this as a cost or an investment?"

Objection: *"We would have to train everyone on this and that would be such a large undertaking!"*

Persuasive Question: "Do you think our employees would appreciate training on a system keeps them current and will make things easier for them in the long run?"

Do you see how this combination of making strong power statements and asking persuasive questions can change the focus of what is being said? Do you see how these questions are carefully crafted to ensure objectivity? The persuasive questions are used to deflect resistance and encourage embellishment and uncover the real truth around the perceived obstacle. The pessimists must explain themselves, in front of the group, which often uncovers a previously hidden fear or issue around change.

My first job out of college was at an advertising agency in New York City. While I was there, I learned a very valuable lesson from the agency's CEO. His name was Ralph and he knew everyone's name in our company of 150 employees. He was always smiling as he walked through the hallways and greeted everyone pleasantly. When Ralph walked into a meeting, he always had his well-formed outcome in mind. He knew exactly what he wanted and how to get it. He would make these power statements – and just sit back and watch everyone in the room churn it out. He would interject, appropriately, with all the right objective questions, that focused on the positive and then he, would again, sit back. Inevitably, someone would say what he wanted to hear. And he would perk up and shout a resounding, "Yes! He's got it! That's it! That's a great idea! Let's do it!" He could have started his meeting 80 minutes ago with, "Here's what I propose"…. Or "Here's what I've decided we're going to do." But he knew how to get buy-in. That's how I learned it. And now you know, too.

Tip: The key here is to float above the conversation, witnessing what is going on objectively rather than to get too involved. Women can become especially good at tapping an observational point of view as we try to understand the different perspectives of group members. Some changes will mean more work for some people in the room, so it's natural for them to show resistance.

Some people may feel inadequate or not equipped to handle what is being suggested, such as feeling technologically inferior or unprepared. The empowered woman should consider the objections from the point of view of fear. (Think, what is the person that is doing all the objecting *afraid* of?) If you can figure that out, you can address it as a general question to the group.   Questions like, "What kind of training would be needed for …..?" or "Who would do all that work?" Asking the right questions of the whole group can suppress the fear of an individual and/or bring out, into the open, the real issue at hand, without pointing any fingers and maintaining the dignity of all involved.

I have also coached my female professionals to use this trick when they feel someone in the room doesn't understand something. Training sessions and prospect meetings can sometimes have people going off on tangents, or explaining something that the empowered woman either doesn't understand herself or feels that a younger staff isn't catching on to etc. Asking that carefully crafted general question is a great way to have something explained without looking stupid.

Give Everyone a Fair Chance to Be Motivated

Another tip for the empowered professional woman to keep in mind, when putting together a team, is to ASK for volunteers. I have said this before – we don't ask enough professionals at work what it is they want. When was the last time anyone asked you what you want? Further, does anyone follow-up with, "How can I help you?" This is a fantastic practice to adopt and it will get you a team like you never would have thought possible. I was coaching a marketing professional who was dejected because she couldn't get approval in the budget to launch a much-wanted Intranet at her company. She knew that the intranet would serve the company well by offering a centralized place for all of her marketing materials, pipeline reporting, news about clients and staff, etc. But there seemed no way to get it off the ground. I suggested she consider putting together a voluntary taskforce. After some consideration she sent out a communication that outlined the well-formed outcome of having the intranet. The language was careful to address the personal gain for the employees and the value it would provide the firm overall. She then called for all interested parties that would want to help build the intranet to meet her in Conference Room B at 2:00. She was pleasantly surprised to meet with seven staff and someone even brought donuts! She was also surprised to find that many of the younger staff, including one of the IT guys and an administrative assistant, possessed the skills necessary to build a highly effective intranet. They were happy to contribute to the firm in a new way that showcased their abilities and happily worked together, launching the intranet in only four months. Admittedly, it was one of the most professional looking and user-friendly intranets I had ever seen, honestly, and to this day it still serves the company well.

4 - Empowered Women At Work...Act Confident

Every day in business there are difficult decisions to be made; they are simply part of the art of the deal.

Sometimes, the deal itself becomes the goal and the details get lost in all of the time, effort and energy put forth just to get to closing. Last year, as we were ramping up our business, an historic tax credit opportunity was presented to us by a major bank. To us, novices with tax investment partnerships, the deal looked like a great and lucrative prospect. I spent a lot of my time, my team's time, a lot of money and a lot of sleepless nights just to get to the finish line even though I didn't feel comfortable with all of the parameters of the transaction.

Mere days before our scheduled closing I could no longer ignore my gut feeling that this was not the right partnership for my company. So during one terse negotiation, I pulled the plug, leaving almost six million dollars on the table. My partner was distraught, my investors concerned. My challenge as a leader was to not only convince them, but also myself, that I had made the right decision.

About six months, and even more sleepless nights later, an opportunity presented itself that not only proved more fortuitous to the company's growth trajectory and bottom line, but which would establish the potential for future business with a national real estate conglomerate.

My investors realized returns 18 months before projected. My partner realized that maybe I did know what I was doing. And, in that defining moment for me, I realized how this situation had honed my trust in my gut instinct.

  - Dana Spain, Managing Partner, McSpain Properties
  President & Founder, PAWS
  Former & COO, Philadelphia *InStyle* magazine

How can you evoke confidence when you have no knowledge about what is being discussed or proposed? No one can know everything or everyone. No one has read every book or has all the answers. But some professionals try to come across that way. After a short while, those who try so hard lose some of their credibility.

We have been speaking about asking important questions to gather information toward problem-solving, collaboration and, generally speaking, change.

Many of the professionals I coach are terrified of being wrong or appearing stupid. Of course, we really should be kinder to ourselves. Human error allows 1.5% error but we don't want that to be us – ever - especially in front of others – especially in front of our boss.

Even the most empowered woman has trouble admitting she doesn't know.

A great tip is to replace "I don't know" with "Tell me more."

I was on a coaching call with a female executive who had just returned from a meeting with a man she described as "A-type, entrepreneurial, very successful". She added, "...he's into lots of different things and he talks all over the place. I just spent over an hour with him and he was telling me about a deal he's working on but I just couldn't follow him. I wanted to interject more but after a while I just felt it best if I stay quiet and let him ramble. It's a shame because he's my client and if I could understand the deals he was involved in I could better advise him."

I advised her to interject with three magic words that encourage people to explain and embellish. Please keep in mind that empowered women at work forgive themselves for what they don't understand and realize the value in admitting when they don't know something. But they also know a trick or two about how to look and act more confident, even when they're feeling anything but. The female executive applied this trick at her next meeting (i.e. "Tell me more about that....") with this entrepreneur and reported she was able to gather a lot more meaningful information from her client. She also could tell he really appreciated her interest in him and his recent dealings.

At work, the empowered woman must address the issue of perceived lack of confidence.

Perception is reality, right? Yes, that is right. There is no doubt in my mind, nor should there be in yours, that the number one obstacle that's keeping women from making as much money as men - and that's holding women back commanding important positions of power and influence in this world – is this: a perceived lack of confidence. If you feel that someone has low confidence you are also deeming them be an underperformer; an underperformer that you can't count on to get the job done. This is not someone who you'd hire or trust with anything really important.

I find myself having the same conversation over and over again with my female professional clients as we start addressing their lack of self-confidence. Self-confidence comes from fear, as does every negative, detrimental emotion, and often ties in with shame. Doubt, guilt, insecurity … I consider these all to be in the same basket.

We can choose to empty our baskets now and carry a lesser load.

In order to do that, I will ask you to recognize a rather simple concept – and hold it higher in your state of awareness than ever before. If you can do this, then I assure you that you will be able to put this issue of confidence to bed. This will be something I ask you to accept as a complete truth. And that is this: we live in a world of duality.

Think about it. For everything in this world – all that we know – has an opposite. Up and down, cold and hot, right and wrong, him and her, day and night, true and false, ebb and flow. Everything has a reflection, an opposite, an opposing perspective. This observation, in and of itself, explains all conflict. It is how our world works. This is the key to answering the big question of, "How do I become confident?"

You can feel completely confident because of the knowledge and acceptance that opposition simply exists in the world we live in.

Maintaining awareness of this simple truth is your next huge step toward being better able to deal with conflict and opposition. If we agree that this is a fundamental truth then we should no longer feel threatened, ashamed or defensive the next time someone disagrees with or challenges us. In fact, we must expect and be prepared for that opposition. Why wouldn't we?

This is really not a big shock to you and I know that. But keep reading because I want to shift your attitude around conflict and opposition. Instead of groaning because we have to prepare for the inevitable opposition, we should be readily and happily prepared for it – preferably, in a non-personal, non-defensive way. The beauty of this approach is when we surrender to the fact that this is the way it is, it encourages us to prepare for – and rise above - the duality.

It's not he said vs. she said, but an understanding and complete acceptance of what both have said.

The Story of MaryAnn

MaryAnn works at regional professional services firm. She is a real go-getter, with high aspirations about her career. She values being visible in her professional community and establishing herself as an expert in her field by building a strong personal brand. As such, she had thoughtfully identified a top-notch organization where she could get involved by sitting on a board, joining committees that would allow her to socialize with other powerful women in her town. She enjoyed her involvement there and was soon thriving by speaking, writing and expanding her connections with professionals that could fuel her career. She was thrilled to be asked to make a half-day presentation at one of the organization's upcoming events that would attract hundreds of local professionals. This would help her achieve that visibility she desperately wanted. One of her senior male supervisors scowled when she asked (yes, it was too bad that she *asked*) for the day off to attend the event. He said something like, "I don't know why you'd want to be involved with that organization." And he shook his head. She was devastated! How could this happen? How could she be so far off in having pinpointed this organization as one she would get involved with? She felt she had made a big mistake and arrived at our coaching call near tears. "I feel really badly about this. I mean, I've put in all this work — and for what? He doesn't want me to be there. I guess I'll resign my position. I'm not sure about the speaking engagement….." Whoa! I reeled her back in. I asked her to remind us both why she was so attracted to this organization, what she loved about what she was specifically doing, how her involvement thus far had helped her. She started to remind herself about all the benefits that she had enjoyed since becoming involved in this organization. She had brought in some leads for her company through her networking there. Her involvement taught her things she needed to know in her line of work and expanded her relationship with several important referral sources. She felt a sense of belonging and was given opportunities to become a better presenter, which would surely fuel her career at the firm. "Wow!" she said as she listened to herself. If I explained this to him, this could totally change his mind. Why didn't I think of that?"

She forgot there, for a second, that we live in a world of duality. It's really this supervisor's right — almost his obligation (using my theory) - to challenge her on her choice; quite possibly to challenge her on all that she does. Also, let's not forget that he is paying MaryAnn a salary and it's perfectly valid that he ask her to explain why she does what she does.

I have coached many female professionals who have been able to re-invent themselves at work.

They identified their self-limiting beliefs around "can't" and "shouldn't" and allowed themselves to embrace a new demeanor. In many cases, they assumed an entirely new role at work, received more money, gotten promoted or left their place of employment for much more gratifying positions elsewhere.

I have spoken about the perfect storm that is whirling around the global workplace. The incredible leaps in technology over the recent past (the last 20 years alone is mind-boggling) has made me view many things with a different point of view.

For those of you who understand even a little bit about programming, you'll see that logic is based on a series of "what if" scenarios, something that I believe also greatly affects our own life experience. Logic would dictate that we should carefully embrace life-altering choices, by considering the impacts of each possibility. A computer program will say, "if this is chosen, then this might materialize…" We can parlay that logic into our life experience. If we choose XXX (a mindset, a value, an emotion, a judgment, etc.) then our experience will be adjusted accordingly. We meet someone and make a choice about how we will perceive this individual – we may either choose to like him or not. And our choice will affect us, surely. This sounds like life, right? What's powerfully significant to me is the actual, pivotal moment of choice - at which everything changes.

Let's look at recent discoveries around quantum physics. We now know that the composition of the smallest particle known to us changes depending upon its observer. In other words, an object's actual composition will change as its observers change. More interestingly, this occurs despite the discovery that at the center of all particles is….well, nothing. This means, truly, that the beauty is in the eye of the beholder, because at the core, there is nothing really there at all – that our observation will create our experience. So, might it be that we are choosing our reality in that moment?

If we choose to see something a particular way, it *is* that way – at least to us. If we can choose to see ourselves in a particular way, then we have the power to create a choice that will impact our actual life experience!

Might the empowered woman be able to choose to step into an entirely different belief about herself which can completely change the course of her career? Further, in that moment of choice, can't she re-direct her life – impacting certainly, her future – but also her historical past?

Think about how three different people come back from a meeting with an entirely different version of what went on:

"Steve was great. He commanded the room."

"My God, I thought Steve would never shut up in there."

"Once again, Bob never spoke up. He always looks so disinterested in these meetings."

(Another true story, by the way).

The empowered woman understands that everyone has a right to make their own choices about how they perceive her. She also understands that she has this choice as well.

I'm suggesting that you can re-invent yourself at any time.

If we believe in who we are, then we are who we believe in. If we believe that we are confident, we are. If we act as though we believe we are confident, we will be perceived as confident. And if we are perceived as confident – then we are... ***confident***. Perception is reality.

How many times have you been re-invented? When you were accepted into your college of choice, when you got married, when you had a baby, when you had the next baby...when you took that job, when you said OK to something risky; in those pivotal moments, not only were you redefined, but your past and future were immediately re-written. The short stories that are featured in the chapters of this book are great examples of how a story is told, using a pivotal moment to explain the re-invention. It's a mindfulness that allows you to witness what happened, in addition to having experienced it. Some professional women have told me that, in focusing on a particular life event, they can re-tell their story as it supported that one occurrence. I experience this when I write resumes or professional profiles for clients. For one particular job, I will tell a slightly different story; for another opportunity, a very different one.

Are you starting to see how our choices, values, desires and goals can and should affect our life experience? We can tell a different story if we want to. After all, we are empowered women!

We all have different stories to tell and we all have different perspectives. We can re-examine our life stories, shift the perspective (make some edits) then embrace and adopt a new version - and step into our new reality at work. I believe that any woman can reinvent herself at any time. I believe that if you want things to be different, they can be. You just have to give yourself permission to succeed on your own terms. Rise above the expected opposition and stop taking conflict to heart. It's a rule of engagement. Expect it, prepare for it. Smile upon it. You got this!

Furthermore, because women are more adept at understanding complex relational systems, quickly and efficiently, and because women excel at reading non-verbal cues (yes, this is also true as a part of brain research) women are very capable of manipulating the perception around how we are perceived.

If you understand how you are perceived at work (ask a few people that you trust to be honest with you) then you should be able to understand why you are perceived that way. Just as you should be able to understand one perspective from someone else about yourself, surely you can adopt an opposing perspective as well. We deny and reject other's perceptions of ourselves all the time. But we really can't, can we? If perception is reality, and they think what they do about us, then guess what? To them, that's who we are.

In my opinion, we choose to see ourselves however we want. In some cases, perhaps we've just chosen a less empowering version of our life story. We can re-write our life story – anytime. When you re-write your story, you can literally step into a whole new you.

5 - Empowered Women At Work...Speak Impeccably

My journey toward empowerment has been slower than I would like, and most likely is still in process, but has definitely centered on learning to speak my truth, to accept myself, and to speak impeccably about the amazing professional that I am.

My journey to become more empowered at work began five years ago. I am a certified public accountant (CPA) and had just completed my tenth and worst ever "busy season." I knew that I would not complete another, yet I felt lost about where to go next. I decided to ask for help and quickly called a local life coach before I could change my mind. I was encouraged to experiment with and give voice to ideas that I had previously left unspoken. I did. I said, "I want to help people. I want to write. I want to be financially successful." For a while, all that I had were these statements, but these statements led me to two seemingly unrelated career opportunities.

First, I landed a part-time position as a campaign coordinator for a major, national health organization. I eventually found myself speaking to crowds as large as 1,200 and doing multiple television interviews. I never knew that I could do this! As a matter of fact, I certainly would have said that I could not do that only a few months before!

Second, I decided to try one master's level English class at a local university. I have since earned my master's in English and had my thesis published. I have now been published multiple times for both my creative and business professional work.

When this journey began five years ago, I could not have imagined that these two paths - not only so different from each other, but also so different from public accounting - would lead me right back to public accounting. I now work as a consultant, specializing in family law and business valuation. I help people through the most difficult experience of their lives – divorce; and I tell the stories of fascinating entrepreneurs in my valuation narratives.

Five years ago I said I want to help people and I want to write. I do this now. I want to be financially successful, too. I have given this idea voice and I know that the success will come; perhaps in a format that I cannot yet imagine, but it will come.

    - Sherry L. Ziesenheim, CPA, CVA, CFF, MA - Financial
    Consultant   Family Law / Valuation / Litigation / Forensics

To speak impeccably means to speak without sin. Empowered women at work are careful to speak what they mean. They are also careful not to criticize themselves or others. That would be sinful. This means that they resist the urge to self-deface by saying things like "I'm such an idiot." Conversely, this means they only choose the high road when speaking about others. They do not gossip and they don't say anything about someone that they would be ashamed of saying in their presence. Empowered women at work choose their words carefully and pay attention to tone, inflection and expressions, when speaking face to face. Research of our brains implies women excel at interpreting communication that is expressed with subtle nuances in inflection and the use of facial expressions. This can help us to instruct, deflect and assist our male counterparts in interpreting the subtleties of important conversations that might affect the outcome for all involved.

Hint: This also means that you might think twice, if you're unsure as to whether your boss picked up on that little hint you gave him through a subtle expression or gesture; chances are, he didn't.

Communication in the workplace is a very important topic and one that I address quite often in my coaching practice. The goal of mastering effective communication is that we get our point across. This is, perhaps, more important than the fact that some professionals are annoyed at the transformation of the English language in a corporate environment – slang, lingo, emoticons, mis-spelled, abbreviated text messages, etc. For the purpose of our exploration here, let's agree to put the rest aside. I would be satisfied with addressing some of the most common issues I see regarding unclear communication in the workplace – which have to do with clarification around a desired outcome, clear expectations, and details – such as when, how, who and why something will get done. I observe many corporate professionals who have allowed themselves to be caught up in routinely rushed exchanges of incomplete thoughts, constant distractions from numerous external factors (and devices), and an urgency to get as much information exchanged in the quickest manner in the briefest amount of time. There seems to be too much time talking for the sake of talking and an uneven amount of focus on the problems, as opposed to the solutions. I also see lots of scheduled, last-minute meetings without agendas, meetings without clear action items/homework, meaningful follow-up or accountability.

Aren't there just way too many meetings, overall?

Are You a Master of Communication?

There are common perceptions that often cause a disconnect in communication between men and women. Since knowledge is power, I'd like to address common complaints that men share with me about women. The goal is to understand these points of contention so we can bridge the gap.

Women talk too much.

I once watched the actress, Halle Berry, being interviewed as part of her promotion of a movie she made about a 911 operator. During the interview, Halle Barry was relaying the story of when *she* personally called 911 to report an alleged break-in at her own house. She was hiding in a closet while being instructed by the 911 operator on the other end of the line to stay quiet until help arrived. But she couldn't. The interviewer played the recording and, sure enough, you could hear her chattering away, despite the warnings of the operator. Her life is seemingly in jeopardy, and keeping quiet under this stressful situation might mean the difference between life and death for her – yet, she remains to talk nervously. Why?

Brain science demonstrates that women tend to talk more when they are under stress. Research shows us that women also, generally speaking, tend to be more verbose than men. Research also shows us that men, because of their own unique brain wiring, are not comfortable with that. Because men can't relate to it, they just don't understand – or value – hearing all those words. If you are communicating with a man, or in a group setting with the majority of men, it might make sense to be aware of that. Next time you are in a meeting, take note of how many more words women use to make their point – especially, the use of filler words.

Empowered women know the point they want to make and carefully deliver statements that do just that. They understand that the words they use carry weight with their male audiences and choose them carefully. One of the most effective ways to get our points across – and get what we want at work – is to use power statements because they are statements that are spoken unemotionally, clearly and concisely and are an effectual way of reaching everyone – especially when we have both men and women in the room.

Women ask too many questions.

Studies have shown (and it's highly probable that you have witnessed conversations like this yourself) that men just don't ask as many questions – about anything – as women do. If you have interviewed men and women for the same job, you will notice that men tend to be more focused on relaying their confidence about doing the job over gathering information about the facets of the job. This has to do with their brain wiring. Men are more likely to accept challenges immediately or react with a resounding "yes" - glad to figure out the details later. Men are naturally more assertive and welcome to risk and challenges. Women tend to be more careful and reserved, careful not to bite off more than we can chew. Men and women are different in this way. Both of these approaches have their pros and cons – as does everything. We have already established that. Although we value asking more questions, it is important to understand how that can be perceived by our male counterparts.

The empowered woman understands this difference and can effectively use this knowledge to handle a delicate balance when she is involved in a negotiation or in competition with a man.

She understands that if there are women involved, they will appreciate her information-gathering skills so she will be sure to ask well thought-out questions. If there are men involved in the discussion, she will be careful to ask a few meaningful questions, but not too many. More important is her acute awareness around active listening and asking appropriate, leading questions on what is being said in the present. She understands that a demonstration of confidence is important to the men in the room. She may choose to make a simple statement such as, "I am the one for the job, sir" or "You can count on me" and seal it with a firm handshake or a wink. (I have seen both men and women wink effectively and find it can be charming).

Women are too emotional.

Emotional attachment to a personal agenda is critical to motivating others. It's something that must be known and understood to close the sale or get anyone to do what you want. Anyone who is successful understands this.

The problem here is not that women speak emotionally or talk about their feelings. The problem arises when the woman's emotions are of no interest to the "other." Addressing what's personal to the "other" is the key. Women tend to be more focused on the emotional ramifications of an action or situation and, as such, they can be at an advantage. It can greatly serve a woman's cause to use her talents of gauging emotions by switching her focus from her own emotional impact to those around her. In that case women should remain emotional – just make sure to get out of your own head and into the head of those you are trying to persuade – or help – or motivate.

I've seen people argue ... "it's just semantics!" Words are very powerful. They can be as sharp as knives and cut deep wounds. They can speak volumes in seconds. They are quite revealing and hold the key to uncovering the obstacle you need to overcome to move ahead. Just think about the difference between the following:

"I wish…."

What are the chances of a wish statement? "I wish I had a million dollars." "I wish I won the lottery." A long shot indeed.

"I hope…"

"I hope I get that job." "I hope I get that promotion." "I hope I can close that prospect tomorrow." Well, it's a little better, implying maybe a 50/50 chance.

"I expect…"

"I expect that I will be that position in two years." "I expect to visit Sweden next summer." These statements seem very likely to happen.

Empowered women at work speak impeccably and choose their words wisely. They have an expansive vocabulary and know how to use the correct word appropriately in order to get what they want. This is because what they want is holds their best intention and serves the greater good, of course.

Choosing the right words is important. Craft your power statements carefully. Memorize your "elevator pitch." Know your value as it is perceived from the perspective of the other and address that in your conversation.

Asking the right kind of questions, active listening and addressing the emotional attachment of the "Other" (the decision-maker, gate-keeper, boss, employer, etc.) is key to connecting with another person and move forward any initiative that is mutually beneficial.

I was on a coaching call with a young man (an up-and-coming professional in his 30s) and I asked him if he reads books. "I only read tweets." he replied. It may come as a shock to you that the majority of my male clients will tell me they don't read books while the majority of my female clients say they do. I will also be forthcoming and share that most of the women who do read books, do not usually ever include a title that will further their professional career or enhance their knowledge in a specific area that relates to their profession.

E-newsletters and blog posts are great, especially if they are focused on your specialty area. But reading more in-depth texts will educate you, keep you current in conversations with clients and referral sources and should also improve your overall communications skills. I worked for a brilliant man who knew so much about everything; it was actually kind of annoying because no matter what topic you brought up, he would know about the subject, and in great detail. Oddly, I noticed an enormous amount of errors in his written communication. I suspect that he might have had some kind of learning disability, perhaps Dyslexia. He used to record his letters and other written reports into a dictating machine for others to type. The reason that I suspect he had a learning disability is because it has been my opinion that people who read a lot overall write and speak well, and they often have a broader use of vocabulary. Please take note:

Empowered professional women:

- Don't mispronounce words (just people's names)

- Properly use grammar

- Properly punctuate sentences

- Have a large vocabulary (and are proud of it)

- Ask when they don't understand a word (or an acronym) – or anything, for that matter, that they don't understand

- Understand the etiquette around different methods of communication that they are engaged in (e-mail, memos, texting vs. phoning, etc.)

When I was young and starting out, my boss asked me to type an e-mail. This was back in a day where bosses actually wrote things out and gave them to their administrative assistants who typed them up sent them on their boss's behalf. He had put in there a "bcc" which stands for "blind carbon copy." The "cc" that is still used today is a flashback from the time when we typed using a typewriter and had to slip in a piece of carbon paper to make a copy of what we were typing. This is ancient now and although, back then, I knew what the "cc" meant, I did not know what the "b" meant. The first time, I will admit to ignoring the "b" and just copied everyone. The second time I saw it, I thought I'd better check on this. Luckily, I had the sense to call for help and dialed a girlfriend who had been employed as an administrative assistant longer than me, in hopes she would know the answer. Well, she told me (you let the "bcc" recipient see the message without the others knowing). Whew! I never got caught on that first one, and I think I was lucky on that one.

My mother told me a story about when she was secretary to an admiral in the Navy. She mistakenly listed the recipients of a document in the wrong order. Because she worked for the Navy, the hierarchy of the officers that were copied was of great importance. She had not listed them correctly and was reprimanded.

If you don't know the etiquette around your methods of communication, ask. You can ask someone outside of the workplace if you can to avoid embarrassment.

I used to work with a man named Stu, who sat down the hall from me, in an office maybe 20 feet away. Not that long of a distance, but we had e-mail and I'd gotten in the habit of e-mailing pretty much everyone. Stu would print out my e-mail, write "Yes" or "No" on it, then walk down to my office and leave it in my "in-box". I figured out that Stu preferred to walk around rather than have me walk down and stick my head in his office. It's what he liked. He was my boss; I honored his preferences.

Empowered women honor the preferred methods of communication from those they work with. In the movie, *Working Girl,* Melanie Griffith finally scores the BIG job with an office. After years of being an administrative, she is now assigned one. (This is because her character gave herself permission to re-invent herself and change her future). The working girl makes the initial mistake of referring to her as her secretary. "I prefer 'assistant'," she is corrected.   She nods and the assistant adds, "Maybe now's a good time to go over what you expect of me," to which the working girl replies, "I expect you to call me Tess. And I don't expect you to fetch me coffee unless you're getting yourself one, too." The young assistant smiles in such a way, that the audience understands that a loyalty and mutual respect has been established between these two professional women. They are empowered in that moment. These might seem like simple things, but clearing the way about how things should work between professionals at work is often not addressed up front, but rather in hindsight, after there has been a problem. Most professionals are not regularly trained or instructed in simple office skills, like refresher courses in English grammar, how to navigate a Windows environment, or education around doing business with other cultures. These are all important things to keep your professionals competitive, knowledgeable and comfortable.

Make a point of telling your underlings what they do right and what you might prefer to be done differently – tomorrow when you go to work. Think about it. Ask them what they would like, too. Check in with your supervisors, too, if you're not sure about how you're communicating. The question could be simple, "Do you prefer me to stick my head in to ask you questions, leave you a voice mail or send an e-mail?" Everyone's different. If you're not sure, ask. This is obviously most important that first week on the job, but consider asking these questions about preferred methods of communication with your clients, vendors, colleagues, etc. - ask all the new business acquaintances you meet.

I also want to briefly touch upon a few issues around the way women are speaking that, according to some strong feedback - from both men and women – could very well keep female professionals from being perceived as a master of communication. I highlight these issues so that you can be aware of them. You might unwittingly have adopted these yourself or perhaps you know a co-worker, especially a younger one, who is demonstrating these issues/trends around speaking. If any of the following describe how you are speaking at work, please acknowledge it honestly and try to control these habits in your professional environment, because I believe any of these are currently seen as a detriment.

Language barriers/accents – I often hear complaints around professionals who maintain a thick accent or who are hard to understand when they are speaking. If you believe your accent is keeping from you moving forward in your position, please consider hiring a speech coach and/or taking some more education in the language in which you are trying to conduct business. Just as you need to understand the cultures of the foreign countries that you travel to on business, paying attention to mastering key phrases, as appropriate – if not, the language in its entirety – is critical if you want to continue your career development.

The volume of your voice – You will most likely not be perceived as a leader or potentially successful if you are soft spoken. If you want to be successful in business, you need to be heard. One suggestion is to watch a You Tube video in the privacy of your home or office and learn how to project your voice so you can be heard. If people are squinting when you're speaking in a meeting, this means you're talking too low.

Up-Talking – I have heard other terms for this but what I am describing is when people make statements that end with the intonation of a question (a.k.a. as a valley girl accent). I see this myself often enough and, admittedly, it does not instill confidence in the person doing the talking. If you're not sure whether or not you are doing this, ask a confidante at work.

Vocal Fry – this is a trend among young women where they speak very low and slowly – often reaching a lower range that makes them sound creaky or raspy. I have observed this verbal pattern often as I have been made aware of this trend and as I'm writing this book. Although I personally do not find this trait to be offensive I include it here for you to be aware of the fact that it does offend some. My research on this trend shows that urban young females actually aspire to those that are speaking like this – it is somewhat of a social status. However, beware: the professional recruiter is not a big fan.

A final tip for honestly assessing how you are communicating is to record yourself while talking – then listen (don't watch).

6 - Empowered Women At Work...Manage Their Time

I saw a coffee mug that says *"You have the same amount of hours in the day as Beyoncé."*

We all get the same number of hours (168 in every week). The question is how do we maximize productivity, creativity and ensure that we get high quality sleep, food and fun?

A female attorney came to me for coaching because she was worn out, disorganized, and unfocused. She complained that one day bled into another and she was struggling with managing her time. She described herself as a "hamster on a wheel." She was desperate to gain more time for herself so she could be productive and re-build her energy.

Our work began with a data collection exercise: just how was this professional woman spending her time?

Asking an attorney to keep a journal of how she is spending time is not the most popular request because many lawyers document their working time in tenth of an hour increments throughout the day. She initially balked at the idea of recording her non-working hours. However, I maintain there is no better way to determine where to carve out time for goals so I encouraged her to track her time with the sole purpose of having her priorities emerge.

In this case, my client was surprised.

Am I really spending an hour a day looking at Facebook? That's seven hours a week. How important is it to me? What else could I do if I cut that in half or eliminate it entirely?

Do I really need to respond to work calls after 6:00 pm? (She decided not to, noting, "The world hasn't come to an end.")

Rather than stopping everything to respond to e-mails (a huge time waster) she started handling them in batches.

Perhaps most importantly, she found the confidence to talk to her husband and boss about offloading some responsibilities. This allowed her to fit in yoga - which quickly led to sleeping better and healthier eating habits. Her husband commented on how great she looked and she had more time with the family once she stopped taking calls at night.

- Dena Lefkowitz, Esq., ACC – Executive and Lawyer Coach at Achievement by Design, Former General Counsel to the Chester Upland School District, Chief Counsel to the Pennsylvania Office of Open Records and appellate advocate before the Pennsylvania Supreme and Commonwealth Courts

As of the writing of this book, the most common form of written communication in the workplace is undoubtedly e-mail which is arguably, the biggest drain on our time at work, as we shift our focus from what we need to do in order to respond to that pesky "ding"! Since the average professional receives hundreds of e-mails each day, I think this might be the largest drain on professionals' time.

My advice? Shut it down.

No one can become an expert at anything or excel at any one activity if they do not allow themselves full immersion in the topic. Who can concentrate with the constant flow of distractions that e-mail fosters? Outlook is the most popular software program for e-mail usage in the current marketplace and the default setting on that program for the frequency at which you will receive messages is …. five minutes. That means you only have FIVE minutes to concentrate on anything before you hear that next "ding." Here's my advice. Shut off the sound; I suggest you do this immediately. Then re-set your settings to much longer intervals. Don't panic. You can always hit send/refresh if you're dying to see who's been e-mailing you. They will flood right in at the hit of a button. But you need to take control of that. Come on…. Stop reading this book, be brave and re-set the default to 30 minutes. You can do this! Five minutes is barely enough time to answer an e-mail; then you'll be answering another. We get caught up, in this way, working "in" our business instead of "on" our business. We get caught up in the doing and forget to take a step back and ask ourselves, "What do I really need to do now that will take me one step closer to achieving one of my goals?" Before you even open up your e-mail in the morning, ask yourself what you should do proactively that will provide the most benefit before you start reacting to everyone else. This is a very powerful first step in achieving empowerment by taking control of your time at work.

I think one of the toughest things about a traditional corporate environment is the restriction around "alone time" for individual professionals in the office. Although management supports taking a full day or two to go to a separate location for a retreat or conference, it may not support your door being shut for four hours or having someone work from home (or someplace else, off-site). How can anyone fully immerse themselves to learn something new or create a think tank environment in order to solve a problem or be innovative? There are certainly exceptions to this and I have seen some very interesting environments that lend themselves to more creativity and innovation, but this is not the norm, for sure. What I'm saying is that most professional women I know do not give themselves permission to remove themselves from the constant distractions that exist at work. They don't disassociate from the wants and needs of others at work in order to focus on the things that will best serve them and those around them. This is a simple matter of shifting one's focus from being reactionary to being proactive.

Of course, this impacts issues around time management. "I don't have enough time in the day!" I hear this very often from women. Time management is, better put, prioritization. When dinner's ready, and the kitchen table is cluttered, it's time (NOW) to clear the kitchen table – or at least half of it (depending upon how many people are sitting down to dinner). So you make the time. Time management is sticking to a list of what's the most important thing to do. It's really prioritization of things that must get done. So how do you prioritize? Usually, women take care of others first. I'm suggesting you try taking care of yourself and your needs first – addressing your goals, because you are in touch with their importance, to your core – and you have an emotional attachment to the impact that can be made once they are achieved. So this is not being selfish at all – this is serving the greater good, from your best, highest self.

You don't have to make an announcement, formally, of this change in you. Others will soon take notice and see the difference in you – in how you are doing things, handling yourself - noticeably different. Let's explore some of the common obstacles, confusing dilemmas that surround this kind of empowerment, shall we?

In order to do this honestly, we will have to remind ourselves of the some of the most basic differences between men and women and how those differences most commonly manifest at the workplace. This will help us to stay focused on how we achieve – albeit, communicate, request, demand, explain, justify – our newfound sense of self.

Let's say you are walking into work, with all the grace and confidence in the world because today is the day you are ready to tackle a strong step in the right direction to get you to that next level in reaching an important goal you have set for yourself. You are going to write a very important piece of communication that will require 90 minutes of your time this morning and you have cleared your calendar. Or you are going to make a few very important calls in this 90-minute period. Or you are going to have a serious discussion with someone…whatever it is, you have set aside this special 90 minutes of time this morning for YOU to do this because you have decided that this is a priority for today and you are ready, willing and able to get this done – TODAY. Now – during these next 90 minutes – and as you glide into work, you smile and greet this person here…. And nod and say "Good morning" over there … and you are walking toward your destination …. when you are called into the open doorway to a conference room with a few of your colleagues in it. They call your name and ask you to step inside. They may even ask you for permission, as I often hear people do. "Gotta minute?" they ask. What do you say? How do you say it? What if two of the people that called you in are technically your superiors? Stop right here. (Has this ever happened to you? Sure it has. Maybe they are above or under you in the hierarchy of titles/seniority – it doesn't really matter here. What matters is that you recognize the common tendency of women to take CARE of any and all who ask for your help. We put others first. It's our strength. It's our weakness. We live in a word of duality and there are pros and cons to every situation.

But this morning, today's 90 minutes. You have only these 90. At 10:30 am your meetings start and that's when you will have to be available to everyone else. Tick….tick….tick…. and if you allow yourself to get sidetracked this morning – AGAIN – well, this is really the root of all the trouble, right? Not enough time to ever get anything done! Right? Wrong. It stops here. Now.

Before you read any further, I beseech you to delve inside and ask yourself a few questions of discovery:

1. What are they asking you for? What do they really want from you?

2. Can you give them what they want – here and now?

3. Can someone else do this (better or instead of you)?

4. Do you deserve your 90 minutes now?

5. How can you politely, objectively, unemotionally (without apology, since you have done nothing wrong and have nothing to apologize for; without making up any excuses, since you have none to make, because you're doing nothing against anyone and therefore have nothing to be excused for or feel guilty about) say…. No, I really don't have a minute – not now."?

In many cases, you might say you'd be honored or even delighted to be asked into the conference room. And perhaps that is the case. But this is considering that we are prioritizing differently and we have that personal agenda that we are honoring to change some things at work in order to have a better overall professional experience. And in order to change things, we have decided to do things differently and we said we'd start today. So what will you say? May I suggest:

Example #1: Gotta minute?

"I want to help but I have something I need to take care of now. Can we talk later?"

Example #2: There she is now. She'll know what to do. Good morning (insert your name here). We have a problem and we need your help. (Awwwww….they need you?!)

"I want to help you – and I will. But we'll have to get together later – sometime today after 10:30 am. I look forward to helping you in any way I can then."

Example #3: Your phone rings.

"Can I see you in my office?"

Why did you answer the phone? This is YOUR 90 minutes (yeah, I tricked you).

In addition to e-mail defaults being re-set, don't forget that most phones can be set to "Do Not Disturb" and cell phone ringers can be shut off.

If you notice, my examples have been 90 minutes. This is a good start. You should be able to work up to three-four hours slots at a time. Greatness is achieved through focus and concentration – and perseverance. Give yourself the time you need to succeed.

I assure you that none of your colleagues will be offended that you held them off. And let's address another common concern. That someone will actually ASK YOU what you are doing – that they will have you explain yourself as to why you are not available to them, your employer, at this very instant. Well, this is when you will have to step into another part of the armor that empowered women at work wear. The Truth. You should not be ashamed to share with anyone what you are about to do. Because, after all, this goal that you have set for yourself this morning, during your special 90 minutes has been well-crafted to serve your personal agenda, which will also aid in the success of those who employ you. You are not, after all, spending this time surfing the Internet without direction or otherwise idly wasting time while on the clock. In fact, I encourage you to share the actions that you are taking on all fronts – telling everyone what you're doing and why is part of the recipe for regularly demonstrating your value to all that will listen. It is a positive affirmation to those around you – and, most importantly, yourself.

Say what you want. Out loud and often. Write it down. E-mail your desires and well-formed outcomes of all you do – in advance. With confidence and conviction. Tell people what you want - and, if you wait and listen, you may get an offer of assistance from them.

One final note about holding off on being so receptive: often you will be pleasantly surprised (in this world of instant gratification) that many of the requests have already been taken care of when you hold off for a while before responding. You will find yourself getting more "Never mind – all taken care of" messages.

Let's say now, that you have completed the important next step in your action plan toward getting to that next step – say it's a promotion or you want to work on a bigger, more important client that is up for grabs, say that it has something to do with your proving yourself to someone – perhaps over and above someone else internally that you will be competing with for that position. Perhaps you will be competing against another service provider and you are trying to woo a new client. Whatever the scenario, you find yourself competing against a male counterpart. You know this guy. He is an "A" type – very outgoing. He always seems confident, he speaks a little loudly, make sure he gets himself noticed, heard at meetings – maybe he's very pushy. He might even make you uncomfortable. And now you have to beat him or prove yourself over him – or something different has to happen. The common problems that will most likely occur, despite all the best intentions, will surely surround communication. We are reminded that men and women have, inherently, very different styles and preferences around communication.

7 - Empowered Women At Work...Embrace Others

My favorite part of a wedding is that awkward moment just before the first course is served. Everyone's had a few drinks and a few crab cakes and perhaps a mini-quiche or two during cocktail hour. The lovely bride and groom have been introduced and the band is set to go.

It's time to dance. At first, the wedding singer practically begs people to take the floor. A collective bashfulness takes shape in the room that rivals a kindergarten class coming together for the first time.

And then what happens? The ladies take the floor. They're always the first ones out there, right? The first people to say "Who cares what they think of me?"

They dance together, a confident group of uninhibited women, enjoying themselves without fear of judgment.

I have to wonder: As women in business, why are we so reticent to put ourselves out there when we need career help or professional guidance? We are relatively quick to pull our friends together to ask about fashion or child care or even appropriate responses to co-workers. So what prevents female CEOs from forming a board of advisors and seeking guidance? In my experience, assistance in all arenas is essential in order to grow a successful business.

Does the actual dance of *asking for help* need to be a soul-crushing admission of weakness?

For many successful women professionals, being a curious sponge for information and remaining open for others input can fuel a successful career. Admittedly, this isn't for some and I know lots of women who find asking for help to be difficult as they don't want to admit that they don't know something. This is, of course, true for both genders in the business world.

As a long-time consultant to the pharmaceutical industry, I'm witness to the fact that women are less likely to come forward with needs and questions than men. And I sit in amazement as to why.

The effects of trial and error can be devastating to the time axis on the learning curve. It makes little sense to go forward blindly when someone right next to you has a piece of advice that could save you a year's worth of effort. It's time to look past our insecurities and identify the advisors we so desperately need. Strike up the band and ask like no one is watching. You might be very pleasantly surprised at the great advice and assistance you receive - and where it comes from.

- Joy Taylor, CEO of TayganPoint Consulting

The average corporate workplace consists of a variety of individuals representing different ages, varying degrees of education, levels of physical fitness, a wide range of cultures and up-bringing, social status, marital status, gender, and religious and political affiliations. In many cases, these individuals would not freely choose to spend as much time together as they do in their work environments. It is not surprising that groups present a challenge.

Awareness of personality types and their related behaviors, such as consistent, predictable reactions to certain situations, is a very valuable tool. It can explain behaviors and improve interactions within the group, support clearer communication, establish agreed-upon procedures, form well-defined expectations, and assist with conflict avoidance and resolution. Understanding your own personality can help you avoid common pitfalls that are keeping your group from reaching its goals. There is no doubt that a leader's personality impacts the effectiveness and productivity of a group so understanding the personalities of the leaders at your company can also enlighten you as to why he does what he does or shy she says things the way she says them. Understanding the personalities of those who supervise you can better help you to communicate more effectively with them and resolve – or better, yet, avoid – conflict.

Some of the most commonly identified attributes of strong leaders are emotional stability, conscientiousness, integrity, and openness to experience, to name just a few. An honest assessment of a leader's strengths and weaknesses can be beneficial in identifying areas for improvement. I often advise, when looking to elect a new leader (such as a president, managing partner or a division manager) to objectively write a job description of the perfect candidate in an ideal scenario *first*, as opposed to coming up with an internal list of potential candidates based upon years of service, reviews, or any other subjective, internal assessments. This way, you can identify the most important traits needed for the job. I encourage conversation and brainstorming about the characteristics of the person you need to attract - as well as the required skill set and experience – including attitude and aptitude. After a careful and honest assessment of the job description, you may now find it easier to qualify individuals in the running for the leadership position.

Example: If you understood that, as part of Joe's personality, he needs time to mull over decisions when he is feeling stressed, it might be better to give him a detailed brief explaining different scenarios surrounding a particular issue and then give him a day or two to make a decision. *If your group, as a whole, will benefit from someone who can make a quick decision, should Joe be appointed as leader?*

Let's say Steve has already been appointed as the leader of a group at your firm. By all accounts, Steve is described as charming, charismatic and extraverted, seemingly bonding quickly with new acquaintances. But Steve has also exhibited a mischievous side, having difficulty taking responsibility for not following up on his promises and a tendency to ignore the expectations that others hold for him. *How should we handle Steve?* After acknowledging this on-going behavior as an issue, one suggestion is to be wary of any unrealistic optimism around his propositions and be sure to have Steve clearly communicate what is expected of him (the trick is to get Steve to say it aloud and/or write it down) on a regular basis, which will help all involved to support his accountability.

Personality Profiling

There are numerous online personality assessment tools that are quick, easy to use and affordable. Accepting and effectively applying the results proves to be the real challenge. In most cases, a personality assessment will identify strengths of an individual as well as areas for improvement. Individuals should be encouraged to explore the results of their personality test in a way that enlightens them about how they are perceived by others at the company. An important step in this process will be to use the results of the personality assessment to applaud what the professional is doing right and also acknowledge areas for improvement in a way that creates an impetus for change (motivation dictates behavior).

Certain personality disorders, such as mental illness, can be revealed during this process. We should acknowledge the overwhelming statistics about the emotional instability that exists in our workforce - depression, passive-aggression, Asperger's syndrome, anger-management deficiencies – are rampant. Many people are on the road on Monday morning chock full of enough pharmaceutical medication to qualify them as "DWI" and these drugs are subscribed to treat a wide variety of illnesses – physical and mental – with all kinds of side effects. To a certain degree, this is a private matter and none of our business – or is it? I have witnessed some very disturbing behavior in the workplace from some individuals that clearly suffered from some form of personality disorder or mental illness. Employers of these folks often are subject to fees for HR consultants, lawyers and long-term detrimental effects on the morale of the employees who have been negatively impacted.

Here are some real life examples of how ignoring personality types wreaked unnecessary havoc in corporate environments:

To hire or not to hire?

I was coaching a male executive through his hesitation around hiring a new female professional. His reported that the company had been satisfactorily using a personality profiling system for all new hires. The company strongly believed in the profiling process and required all managerial candidates and above to take a one-hour assessment to gain insight into prospective employees. The woman being considered for hire was highly recommended by a member of their management team who had previously worked with her. The male executive shared he was not very confident about the decision to hire her, despite her having the appropriate experience, level of education and salary requirements that all seemed perfect for the position. I asked him why. He blamed the results of her personality profile. "She's just not like the rest of us!" he said.

I explained to him that the best use of this personality profiling system was to learn more about her management style, work ethic, her natural abilities of problem-solving and to try to predict how she might behave under stress. The test was not being done to attract a team of the same, like-minded workforce. We eventually shared a good chuckle over that.

The Funeral

Take the case of a male executive who was not known for his "warm and fuzzy" side. Despite full awareness of his shortcomings in the area of emotional intelligence, somehow he wound up handling the communication of the death of a long-time employee to the staff. He waited until the end of the company picnic to send an e-mail out. He also forgot to send flowers to the funeral home.

This did not go over well.

The Meet & Greet

I was working with a corporate client who was arranging a "meet and greet," as I call them, with another firm that also provided services for their shared target audience/clientele. I prompted my client to conduct some research on who would be coming from the other firm. We looked each of them up on the Internet – perusing their social media profiles as well as the bios on the company website – to gather as much information on their skills and personalities as we could. We hand selected complementary professionals from our side. We even identified two former athletes and made sure that was mentioned as they were introduced to each other. Despite an age and gender difference, this bond between them proved very valuable. The older male former athlete was a more established professional who served the construction industry and the younger female up-and-coming professional was also looking to serve the same industry. He sent her a book he had written the next day and a natural, beautiful mentorship was born.

Not all women are well-versed in emotional intelligence - and some men are. Understanding the short-comings (let's use the term areas for improvement) of under-developed – or non-existent - emotional intelligence of personnel can be very helpful.

I have coached very few men who cited developing their emotional intelligence as a priority.

I work with some female professionals for whom this area does not come as naturally as they would like. The difference is that not only do they see this in themselves, they value learning more in this area because they know it's important. It is especially important for managers to understand how their management style affects the daily experience of those they manage. Another way to enlighten managers is to conduct performance reviews with their subordinates – as opposed to their peers (peers are often subconsciously competitive and can't help but give more harsh ratings).

Empowered women consider all aspects of the personalities of her team

– when she's forming her team as well as managing her team. She knows especially how to carefully consider all those around her in order to most effectively manage her relationships.

When selecting the members of her team, the empowered professional woman considers who will work well together and why. She considers the complimentary attributes that team members possess. One linear thinker can help to offset a loftier, big-picture thinker and the introvert might work well being paired with someone who can help to bring him out more. This can happen when an objective statement about the well-formed outcome is made. "I think that you two will complement each other because of your different styles and approach to this problem. Do you think you can explore and leverage that together?" And, "I expect that you two will both contribute to the preparation and presentation of the material for the client at the meeting next week."

The Art of Mirroring

Another tip that I want to share that will help you to embrace others in a meaningful way is the concept of intentional mirroring. Mirroring is a way of reflecting another so they see themselves. You literally have them see and/or hear themselves through you. The goal is to have someone be able to more deeply understand what their desire or intention is. It is a very effective aspect of coaching – and works wonders when dealing with kids and elders – and anyone else with whom you may have trouble understanding or relating with. It works on the grouchy boss, the brooding teen and the angry spouse. It also works for salespeople, counselors, life coaches and food servers. On a most simple scale, let's use the food server in a restaurant as an example.

I will admit that when I go out to eat, I am apt to make some sort of special request of my server, such as "iced tea, but hold the lemon, please"? or "can you go light on the sauce or put it on the side, please?" etc. A good food server will always repeat the entire order to the table, reiterating all the special requests. And when they do, I always feel so much better. I feel like I have been heard and I like that I am being paid attention to – this food server is taking good care of me and I make a point to give a good tip. In truth, since usually someone else serves the food these days, there is less of a guarantee that all my requests will actually be honored; for instance, it's still about 50/50 chance that I will still get the lemon with the iced tea BUT it's a good start. That, at a very simple level, is the art of mirroring.

Mirroring is a good tactic to use on someone who is speaking negatively about something, making an objection or shooting down an idea. It can also be used to lighten someone's mood. Let's take mirroring one step further and see how this high-level, well-intentioned use of manipulation works on a cranky boss or a moody teen. Your boss comes into a meeting with a stern look on his face and plops down in a chair with a grunt. He is clearly not in a good mood. You feel your stomach sink a bit – you worry, "This might not be a good meeting." You start to feel yourself tense up. You clear your energy and take a breath. "Good morning, Jim," you offer. Look him in the eye and hold your gaze… give it a few seconds. You might even ask, "How are you feeling this morning?" Wait until he offers you something. He might say, "Jeez! The construction on the street outside is intolerable! I hear this project will go on all summer! I just can't stand wasting my time in traffic!!" Avoiding offering any information on the topic or trying to in some way solve his problem – for instance, you wouldn't want to say anything like, "Yep, it will go on for six more weeks." Or "You should try to take an alternate route." Or "Maybe you'll have to start leaving earlier in the morning." Just simply mirror what Jim is saying to you back at him – plain and simple – without anything personal from you. "You're fighting that traffic every day, eh?" or "I can see that the road construction is causing you some serious grief." And if he is being loud you can be loud, too – that's part of mirroring, too. It's a complete absorption of them – bounced off of you – reflected back on them.

The teenager who comes home from school fighting tears in his eyes. You offer, "You OK?" He mumbles, "You wouldn't understand." You fight the urge to come back with something like, "Of course I'll understand. I was a teenager, too once ya know!" Instead you say quietly, "You don't think I'll understand." And you wait...

This technique is a truly terrific way to get everyone to open up. It's so simple yet it requires a heightened sense of awareness, to fight the urge to respond with our ego and, instead, to decide to consciously connect with theirs. Try it – you'll like it – it works.

The Story of Cynthia

Cynthia sat outside the large, corner office of her male department head, seated at a small workstation. At this sales-driven company, employees spent most of their time on the phone. Cynthia was a very religious woman, a devout Catholic of Spanish descent. Since she was fluent in Spanish, she often handled calls from Spanish speaking co-workers and clients. The male department head spent the majority of his time, too, in his office on the phone with clients and colleagues. One of the attributes of this man was that he used foul language – a lot.

Cynthia was appalled as she listened to her boss often scream "F-Bombs" throughout the day. She said one day he couldn't find his notepad and he started screaming, "Mother F....!" Cynthia couldn't take it anymore. Somehow, it was left to me to tell him he needed to curb his use of profanity in the office. He said, "Ah, I'm sick of listening to her speak in Spanish all day long. Makes me think she's complaining about my "f...in" cursing all the time. Just have her move..." Several hours later.... Cynthia got a bigger workstation farther away from her boss's office.

Should empowered women tolerate – or use – profanity? And if so, which expletives are appropriate, which are not, and why?

Cynthia's story comes from New York City, during the 80s and occurred at an advertising agency. It was also a competitive, sales-driven environment. Different companies have different climates and various levels of tolerance around certain behaviors. Over the years, I have personally witnessed a lot more men than women use profanity freely in a corporate environment. I have seen some men apologize when doing so in front of women, but have never seen them apologize in front of other men. Is this a double set of standards or is this an old-fashioned practice of chivalry that hasn't gone away yet? Would you agree that professional women are looked down upon for cursing or is it tolerated and acceptable at your place of employment? Personally, I have found it can be quite effective to use a choice word selectively for impact – once in a while….when you really need someone (man or woman) to know you mean business. As an empowered woman, you understand that words are powerful and you are careful to use the ones that will get you what you want – because you know what's best for you and what you want is also serving the greater good – your colleagues, your company, and/or humanity.

The truth is we are all very different people. This holds true for those of us in and out of the office. The world is a wonderfully diversified place and I am enjoying seeing a tighter world-wide understanding of different ethnicities and cultures come together in a global marketplace. You might want to consider these cultural and ethnic differences when selecting a client service team or putting together a team to meet with a prospective client. You might find yourself with an opportunity to more purposefully hand pick a small group of your professionals to attend a networking event. Careful attention to the personalities of the individuals that will be present can help form a stronger strategic alliance. Consider who will be in attendance from the other side and try to match the individuals accordingly. This can help build rapport and help you stand out from your competition and ensure a smoother relationship moving forward. Think gender, age, political affiliation, religious beliefs, marital status, sexual orientation, hobbies and personal interests. Everything we're not supposed to consider, right? It is human nature to gravitate to others just like us. There is an enormous amount of interesting research on the subject of subconscious bias. Long story short, we prefer to be with others just like us. We can pretend these similarities don't matter and not openly acknowledge this, but if you want to be empowered at work, you will certainly consider this. After all, it is either a problem or not, that we are different. If we are judging and/or criticizing someone just for being different, that might be a problem. But if we are simply identifying these subtle nuances around what makes us different – just as we objectively assess different personalities types that make us work well together, than where is the problem? Perhaps our approach on this should be more of an acknowledgement of our similarities rather than our differences. Knowledge is power and we want to know how men and women think differently and why they act differently – not to judge their behavior and attitudes - but to better understand them and find ways in which to support each other and work better together.

I often recommend forming strategic alliances with other, like-minded businesses who offer different products and services to the same group you serve. This way, because you touch so many of the same prospects and clients, you can start to recognize potential needs or issues they are facing and offer help to them. In this way, you can satisfy your customers' needs or address your clients' issues in a way that makes you their hero – while securing a referral arrangement with other cool professionals like you. Many professionals understand this yet still struggle with maintaining meaningful relationships with referral sources. I suggest that we embrace the personalities of those referral sources with whom we choose to work with and pick only those that we have something in common with. Young moms, basketball coaches, bitter divorcees – whoever we are - should commiserate together. Having fun with your chosen referral sources and vendors makes work fun!

I search everyone before I meet with them on-line and you should, too. I have found a wealth of information about people that has helped me to bond with them quickly and ask appropriate questions that help to strengthen our relationship. I strongly suggest you do your research in this way and, in fact, use the Internet to help you to select those you wish to network with – not the other way around. Empowered professional women are proactive and smart as they build their network.

8 - Empowered Women At Work...Respect Themselves

At my first marketing job, I encountered one of the firm's few female partners. I admired her for her intellect and for "making it" in a man's world. She was not only smart, she was an impeccable dresser and had this flaming head of red hair, which only made her tall stature seem that much larger and authoritative. She spoke eloquently with formality and purpose. When she spoke, you listened.

But she could also be hurtful and insensitive. During my regular marketing presentations at the partners' meetings, she often questioned me with cutting remarks such as "This report is inconclusive" or "this makes no sense." I often found myself explaining and defending myself, only to have her snap "...well, you should have put that in your report!" She would *always* seem to find some fault with my reports.

Shortly after having our first son, I attended a company picnic. I was trying to lose the pregnancy weight and remembering feeling less than attractive at that time. Elizabeth commented, in front of all the employees, "So you are still eating for two?" This comment threw me over the edge. With tears in my eyes and humiliation in my heart, I ran to the restroom for a good cry.

I decided that these offensive remarks from Elizabeth needed to end. I was going to set a time and meet with her privately and tell her how I felt.

Elizabeth was 20 years my senior and quite accomplished. I was new at the firm and a rookie. Elizabeth had a tough exterior and I was afraid of her. But I went ahead and scheduled a private meeting.

I was able to hide my fear from her and gathered all my courage as I spoke to her from the heart. I told her that I knew she was a kind and thoughtful person and would not want to hurt anyone, but that I felt hurt by some of her remarks and I shared those remarks with her. She appeared surprised and taken aback. She assured me that she *was* a kind and thoughtful person and did not realize that her remarks had hurt me.

This private conversation changed our whole relationship and from that point on, she treated me with a new respect. I have continued to stand up for myself ever since.

- Jill Lock, Director of Marketing, Isdaner & Company

The Story of Kathy

Kathy greeted me with an almost panic-stricken tone asking if she could re-schedule our coaching call because she had "…a huge report that I have to do and I've had no time to do it and there's been so many distractions and even though I have so much to discuss with you, I don't see a way….." I interjected by saying we could just talk for a few minutes but could I just ask her a couple of questions. She agreed. We spoke for the full session and at the end she had discovered a few very revealing things about herself. She was taking herself for granted, putting others' needs before hers. As a result, her work product was suffering, she was feeling drained and exhausted and her clients were being neglected. What was the real culprit? She had not put herself first. The report that she needed to provide to her client required at least 90 minutes of solitude, so she could research some data, formulate her thesis and write up meaningful recommendations. How could she manage this with her door wide open, people coming and going, chit-chatting, stopping her train of thought to ask her questions? How could she focus with the phone ringing and the e-mails coming in steadily at nearly 300 a day? It's no wonder the woman was so frazzled!

Some of our conversation went like this: "I understand that the hurdle around getting this report done is not so much the time needed but your ability to focus on only this report. Is that right?" She agrees. "So how much time do you think you'll need to complete the report if you were completely undisturbed and not distracted?" She replied that she estimated she would need approximately 90 minutes. "Okay, great. 90 minutes. Will you be there in the office for the next 90 minutes then?" She said yes, the office is where she would be for the rest of the day and it was 1:00 pm at the time. "OK, then let's have you give yourself the 90 minutes you need to get this report done, ok? How would you feel if this report were completed today before 3:00 pm? Would that feel good?" I asked. "Oh yes, that would positively make my day!" she replied. I asked her if she could shut everything else down while she worked on the report. She was very resistant. She cited her open door, the phone and her incoming e-mails as the biggest obstacles. Three obstacles to overcome, I observed.

Number one obstacle – the door. "Can you shut your door?" I asked. "Oh, no, I couldn't shut my door", she replied. I asked her why. "We don't do that here. No one shuts their door." "No one?" I asked. "Are you sure that **no one – *ever*** – shuts their doors for any period of time?" Long pause. "Well, yes, there are a few guys who do … who have, on occasion, shut their doors." "So, can you give yourself permission to shut your door for 90 minutes?" I ask. Pause. "Well, I don't know. They'll all be thinking about what I'm doing in here." "Wow! Really?" I asked. "You must be really important!" We both laughed. She shut the door.

Number two obstacle – the phone. "Is there a Do Not Disturb button your phone?" I questioned. It took a minute or two but she found it. After a few more nudges and questions of discovery, it was finally decided that it would be okay for her to press this button. We even put a post-it note on the phone as a reminder to turn it off when the report was finished.

Number three obstacle – the e-mails. "Did you know that Outlook comes with an automatic default of how often your inbox is flooded with new messages?" I questioned. She was shocked to realize that the factory default setting was 5 minutes. "I had no idea but I guess that makes sense," she said. I encouraged her to take a look at the messages in her inbox from that morning. "Were any of them really requiring an immediate response?" "No. not really," she admitted. Not only did we agree that we could go without reading these e-mails for 90 minutes we reset her default to 30 minutes. I have brought up this issue of constant e-mails earlier and I strongly encourage you all to take the leap and make this change. I know some professionals who have cut their time to reading messages down to two or three times a day. Often you will find in a large corporate environment, where so many group e-mails are exchanged, that many of the requests that occur via e-mail can be resolved before you responded. I acknowledge that every corporate culture is different, and I'm in no way suggesting that you be unresponsive, but the recommendation of changing the receipts of messages to every 30 minutes is, in my opinion, perfectly acceptable. And remember, you can always hit the refresh button to bring them bring in those messages manually, immediately. My client also made the change to have messages come in without sound.

The result was that – you guessed it - the report was completed. She missed no urgent calls or e-mails. No one remarked that she was behind a closed door, either. She was so proud of herself!

How much of your day is spent rapidly responding to e-mails that can wait? Do you ever take the time to unsubscribe from those annoying, recurring e-mails? (I find that retail stores are the worst.) Most broadcast e-mails that you are getting in daily or weekly will offer you the option of changing your frequencies of being contacted, or give the option of opting out. But you have to scroll down to the end of the message and look for tiny or fainted out print to find the link to unsubscribe. Sometimes, it just seems better to hit the delete button. I encourage you, on a monthly basis, to reset these settings and unsubscribe. You'll be glad you did. It feels good and it does diminish the distractions.

Note: Some companies have different cultures around closed doors. I have worked in environments where it was common for someone to knock gently on doors of those professionals who were working behind closed doors. Usually, this was to drop off something they had asked for or to leave a phone message, etc. If you were to open a door to find someone immersed in thought or nose deep in a book, it is hoped you would have the common courtesy to just step back and out. Options are also to put up a sign asking to not be disturbed until 2:00 pm, etc. If someone is abusing the behind door policy, just have a discussion about expectations. Don't limit yourself by thinking there is only one way to work at your office.

I have so many stories about what goes on in offices, how to get an office, get a better office. Perhaps one of these stories can help incite you to make a positive change around your office.

Karen's Office

Karen was a lawyer who hated her office. She was too close to co-workers. It was too noisy and the distractions were keeping her from getting her work done. Through my questioning, she revealed that there was an empty office on a higher floor that was removed from all the hustle and bustle. We explored the obstacles around her moving into that office until she was resolved that it was okay for her to move into the office. She made a statement to the office manager about her moving to that office (rather than asking if she *could* move into the space). She knew what she wanted (her goal was to move into that office) and instead of asking, in this case – she simply stated it. Karen was only able to do this after she explored all the obstacles and presuppositions of her doing so – asking herself what would other people would think of her if she moved her office (did it matter to anyone and if it did, maybe they would admire her for making a change that suited her), and she was able to finally give herself permission to get what she wanted. She was shocked that she was not asked to defend her statement about moving her office. She was asked why she wanted to move there. She explained her need to be more removed from distraction so she could get more work and this was readily received, without question. They even helped her move! She reported getting more done verbally around the office shortly afterward, proudly.

Staci's Office

Staci wanted an office but didn't have one. She went on and on to me about all the reasons she should have one (she dealt with confidential material, she often had sensitive conversations with employees, her neighbor in the open work space was bothersome, etc.). I asked her if there was an office that she could move into. I asked her if she had shared any of this information with anyone else. I discovered that she had not told anyone she wanted an office, or that she had one identified or why she felt she needed a private office. Because she convinced herself that her request was a viable one she finally did ask the appropriate person at her company for the office. She was unemotional, convincing and confident in her request. Staci also got her office and was helped to move.

Margaret's Office

Margaret's office was moving into another location. She came to one of our coaching sessions very upset because someone else had made a remark that implied she would be losing her own office in the move. She spent a great deal of time worrying and plotting about how to avoid losing her office. She was encouraged to ask to see the plans for the new office, which turned out to be publicly available for all to see – on the blueprint was her name written where her new office would be – in a lovely location. She was very happy. So much for listening to office gossip.

I'd like to address women's overwhelming need to being reactionary.

Women aim to please and are often too quick to react. To respond. To take care. To fix. We need to step back and ponder. My advice? Stop saying yes. Don't say yes to anything anymore – yes, that's what I am suggesting. Don't say yes to the invitation to lunch, don't hit accept to the meeting invite, and don't say "OK" when you really don't want to. It doesn't serve you - it keeps you from achieving your goals, hitting your deadlines and diminishes your credibility and reputation. So please stop doing it. You do not need to reply to e-mails when you get them. You do not need to chair every committee and you should not attend any meeting or luncheon without a well-formed outcome. I would rather that YOU do the asking out to lunch, and you send out the meeting requests – with agendas please – and that you are more proactive around all that you do. My hope is that you will change from being reactionary during most of your day to just being pleasantly surprised once in a while. You should have a well-plotted day each and every day with reasonable expectations. At the end of your day, you should feel good about what you achieved and content with your progress. This is how empowered women work – on the job and in life. Some of you will have to ease into this new role of not being so available. Power statements that hold others off until you are sure are, as follows:

"I'm not sure."

"I'll get back to you on that."

"I'm still on the fence."

If you don't want to face them here and now to tell them no, then by all means, stall them and then hit that easy button and say no later in an e-mail or a voicemail.

If you are nervous about asking a referral source out to lunch and you feel it should be done via phone, try waiting until after hours and reading a scripted message for their voicemail. This trick is good for selling to clients and other difficult conversations that you have to have professionally.

Always press the easy button whenever possible!

As you get more confident about the things you want, asking for them or making objective unemotional statements get easier. Additionally, as you realize that you are starting to get what you want, you will become ever more courageous and even start to enjoy this process!

One of the best tips I ever learned from my mother was to not ask permission for things I wanted, but rather to make simple statements at work. "If you ask if you can leave early, they might say no," she warned. I had a boss once say to me, "Just tell me what you want and why, don't ask me anything." I loved that boss. It was like he came with instructions!

I witness many professional women asking other professionals how they should do something. Empowered women do things the way they should be done – as opposed to how someone else wants them. Making recommendations as to how things should be done, from more of a universally beneficial perspective rather than a personal one, will help you stand out from the rest and elevate you to being seen as a leader and innovator. Avoid asking questions like "How should I do it?" but ask rather what is wanted. Pay attention to tone and how you refer to yourself and your work product. "What the most important information you want compiled?" rather than "How should I organize the data?" Don't start questions with:

"Should I…?"

"Can I…?"

"Is it alright if I….?"

"Can I ask you a question…?" (you could have already asked it by now)

Words are important. So are how you use them. The rule of thumb is that the tone and emphasis should be around the well-formed outcome, not the people involved in it. That's key in everything you manage at work. We will talk more about communication later in the book.

I have a confession to make. During most of my adult life as a professional, first as a regional business manager for a national advertising company, then as a marketing director at a professional services firm, and currently as the president of my own company, I have always maintained another secret job. I have been a group fitness instructor since young adulthood. For me, it was motivating to be employed in this way because it kept me exercising, I enjoyed the environment, it challenged me to grow in a variety of ways and I get a little pocket money (very little, honestly). This might not be a big deal to most of you. But you might be surprised to hear when I exercised. I did it at lunchtime. For many years, I excused myself to go and teach classes down the street – and in one instance, we had a gym on the premises. The tricky part was keeping it within the constraints of an hour – which I couldn't do. So I didn't. I didn't come in early and I didn't stay late. I usually left my corporate jobs a bit earlier when I commuted by car because I find sitting in rush hour to be a frustrating waste of time. I was able to convincingly communicate to those who asked why I did what I did. On my own terms. My bosses changed, and one or two co-workers made a snide remark or two, but I never missed a beat. And I never felt guilty. I was a productive employee and made a point of sharing my accomplishments on a regular basis with all who care to hear them. I always was where I needed to be in a most professional manner. I conducted myself with an air of confidence and my "can do" attitude allowed me a work schedule that perfectly suited my life style and was very rewarding. I will say, if you've never allowed yourself to consider exercising at lunchtime, think again! It's so great to have it done with so you can enjoy your evenings! It keeps you healthy (and therefore, a better performer on the job) helps you sleep better, and keeps you looking great in stylish professional clothes!

First Impressions Last a Lifetime

Remember that empowered women look professionally stylish. Please do save enough money to invest in at least one pair of expensive black slacks and one dynamite suit. If you are a professional woman, please dress that part. You'll feel more successful, you'll be perceived as more successful and, as a result you'll be treated as more successful – therefore you WILL be more successful. Dress for success, always! And if you don't know how to, ask someone who is objective to compare you to a professional successful woman. I always look at first ladies of American presidents. Currently, I am emulating Hillary Rodham Clinton and Oprah. National news anchors like Diane Sayer and Barbara Walters are good, too (as opposed to some of the outfits I have seen on the female news anchors at local news stations which I think are pushing the envelope). Empowered women do not dress sexy at work. Looking good does not mean looking hot. Please go to appropriate retail chains or ask other female professionals that you think look good at work where they shop. Then save your money or open a charge and have at it. Use the sales help, too. Try new looks and ask for feedback.

Being objective is a major challenge in becoming an empowered woman at work. It's important to be able to objectively see yourself through the perspective of others at work. This will enable you to understand your value. After you understand where and how you are valued on the job, you can better communicate and demonstrate that value on a regular basis. You can't value what you don't understand, so if your boss or the powers-that-be (those who will decide or have influence over what percentage your raise will be next year or whether you should be considered for the promotion) don't know how great you are at what you do – then that's YOUR FAULT.

Work isn't where you go, it's what you do.

Recently I toured a work environment at a facility near my home that was mostly empty. I asked, "Where is everybody?" and was told that most of the staff was out serving clients, meeting with referral sources or working from home. I made a face and he said, "I know. We planned for growth and negotiated a 10-year lease. We don't need all this space now, but we're stuck with it." See? A lot has changed in the last 10 years.

Working remotely can save everyone money on gas, time spent on getting ready and the commute time, rental costs of the employer, and time in general. How many hours a week are spent in idle chit-chat or gossip where you work? Of course, in order for there to be productivity while working from home, a certain work ethic must be maintained. I do know people who say they work from home and do not put in full days. But most people do not really put in full days at work – and by this, I mean eight hours of total, honest and completely productive time in work, only working. Really.

The gauge on this is the same - reviews, accountability, and feedback from others. Just like you gauge someone's productivity or efficiency while they come to work every day, you gauge the same if they are working remotely – either partially or full-time. My point here is that of course, this should be an option. It can also, for some businesses, open up to new geographic locations, as you offer employees different time zones for marketing or client service. It also allows people to honor their natural biorhythms. Everyone peaks at different times during the day. I work with one successful female professional who runs her own business. She is a night owl and has rescheduled her workday to suit her needs. She has given herself permission to do so, with great results. When she was stuck in an office, she says, forced to show up at 8:30 am, she was listless and unproductive until after lunch. Now she sleeps in and works til 2:00 am, often. I believe that if we don't address this issue and offer flex time and working remotely, I predict we are going to lose a lot of our professionals at some point. The generation of youths that are in school now, I think, will demand it. So we better starting getting ready now.

I encouraged Pat to open up the dialogue about this with her HR professional and send her some supporting research. Corporate America is going to lose a lot of professionals with policies like this in place. If you are reading this and you are a woman of stature at your firm, please look at some of your policies with discernment. Encourage your HR professionals to extend a survey about some of these traditional policies and rules that might no longer serve the modern generation of staffers. Flexible time, working remotely from home and using skype are genuine possibilities around conquering productivity issues.

9 - Empowered Women At Work...Demonstrate their Value

Demonstrating your value is the key to opening doors that completely change your career and your life.

Ten years ago, I was overworked and stressed out. As the marketing director for a Top 100 Accounting firm, I was working 80+ hours a week, catering to the requests of 40 partners, and spread way too thin. I was stuck in a "no-win" situation and felt completely undervalued.

Then I did something that I'm sure will surprise you - I took on even *more* work.

I was asked to provide marketing consulting to one of our paying clients. I knew I was considered "overhead" by the accountants at my firm because I, unlike them, was not billable, so I was eager to demonstrate my value by showing them my expertise was worth a high hourly rate, too. The partners were pleased I accepted the engagement and I jumped right in.

The client turned out to be a group of marketing-savvy leaders in the accounting profession planning to expand their existing consulting services with a high-profile, sophisticated national conference. As we collaborated, I witnessed an elevation of my professionalism, confidence, and ability to think outside the box, offering strategies and ideas that had been proven outside of professional services yet never offered before to the accounting profession. My ideas were unique and this group of forward thinkers appreciated everything I had to give – so I gave even more. We were creating something special that would prove to be a game-changer for the profession and I was becoming recognized as a big thinker and innovator.

But the real impact came when this client project turned into a career opportunity. The board offered me the job of overseeing their annual conference and becoming its Executive Director – and I enthusiastically accepted. I was able to negotiate an ideal employment situation in the process – working from home, keeping manageable hours and increasing my hourly take home pay. I significantly reduced my stress and was able to start my family and transition to the next phase of my life. What had seemed impossible was now a reality: I was able to finally manage a work/career fit that suited my situation. The most important part? My efforts and tenacity gained enough credibility and respect from the board to be able to work on my own terms. They told me, "We trust you to do it right."

- Kathy Sautters – Director of Communications, Prime Global – An association of independent accounting firms

You can't value what you don't understand.

Here I shall raise a very common problem that I witness with female professionals. They do not communicate their value in ways that others understand. This is not just a women's problem, of course. If we would take the time to objectively address all that we do on behalf of our clients, they would never question our bills. If we would track all of our accomplishments at work on a regular basis, I'm sure we would value our own contribution more. And if we shared those accomplishments with our bosses on a regular basis, they would certainly appreciate us more.

Yet, this is what I see all the time: Corporate professionals wait around for their annual review, and just walk in, hopeful and slightly optimistic that they will be deemed favorable and maybe even be given a raise. Thankfully, this disempowered mindset has been changing as more companies adopt best practices of self and upward reviews. Overall, though, most have given up all control as to how we are perceived regarding performance. Isn't it our responsibility to tell our employers – our clients, our referral sources – what a good job we are doing?

Who's fault is it really if you are overlooked for the promotion or don't get the big raise this year? If you don't get what you want at work, it's either because you don't deserve it or the powers-that-be don't know you deserve it. Why should we expect our bosses, who are caught up in their own personal agendas at work and too busy to take notice of all that we do, to step up and fight for us? They have no real idea what we're up to or the value that we provide each and every day – and it's our responsibility to tell them.

> *Empowered women are quite aware of their contributions to their employers and make strides and track success stories.*

I encourage all my clients to stop DOING anything for 20 minutes every two weeks (I always found Fridays at 3:00 pm to work for me) and write up a short list of bulleted items of accomplishment to send to my boss. This practice works for informing (and impressing) clients, too. Regularly demonstrating your value in a way that meets the perspective of the other will keep you feeling good about yourself and be a tremendous help come review time. And when it comes time to update your resume, take that document out again and look at all that you did over the last year! Some examples of what I refer to as accomplishments, in case you were wondering, are:

- Solved a problem for a client that resulted in a credit of $270

- Intervened on behalf of an intimidated associate who felt berated by a colleague; my facilitation of a discussion resulted in two satisfied, unified co-workers

- Worked remotely from home over the weekend in order to complete the project

- Negotiated savings with a vendor, reducing the cost of the contact by 10%

Please be sure to demonstrate the *value* or *benefit* from the activity, as opposed to just reporting the task or activity that was completed. It is important to be careful that you are not sharing just activities that you did to your direct reports.

"I spent two hours watching YouTube yesterday afternoon" might raise eyebrows. Sharing, more specifically, "I learned about alternate methods of conducting a business valuation from watching a video series; I will now be able to offer several new reports at the upcoming board meeting" is a much better way to communicate that activity. (True story, by the way).

Monitoring your accomplishments regularly will also make you more aware of any necessary improvements you should be making to contribute in a meaningful way. If you decide to share your successes but don't have anything to report, let this be a red flag for you. Everyone has a slow period or takes a vacation but if the months are passing and you've got nothing to show for it, I suggest you ask yourself some serious questions and engage in some soul searching. Empowered women strive to learn and grow and thrive in all aspects of their life.

Discussing your successes with subordinates can improve their loyalty to you and improve morale. Additionally, sharing accomplishments with colleagues can showcase you as a leader and inspire more professionalism at your organization. This is how women learn how to succeed from each other. Examples include:

"I met my client for lunch today and afterward, I helped her pick out a watch." (Really? Is that something we should be doing with clients – go shopping after lunch? Fun!) Note: This was a bonding experience between the service provider and the client and fostered true rapport between them. This is very different from texting with someone outside the office for a half hour during work hours.

"I had a great meeting with a prospect today. My team showed professionalism and were very persuasive. I did a nice write-up on the experience and sent it over to management, the referral source and submitted it as a story for the company newsletter next month."

"One of my vendors expressed concern at his upcoming carpel tunnel surgery because he is worried it will negatively impact his golf game. I found an article on the Internet about how this type of surgery can actually help golfers and I sent it over to him to ease his mind; he seemed very grateful and appreciative."

Women have a tendency to expect others to see all that they do, especially their male supervisors. But they won't. Men's brains work completely differently and they are preoccupied with themselves and their own problems (the truth is, most everyone is). They are not that concerned with you and what you're doing. Until maybe review time – and here I will be brutally honest. I have had many male professionals confess that they really don't spend the amount or quality time they should when reviewing their professionals. This is because of a number of factors and it often has a lot to do with the fact that they have been given too many people to review in too short of a time and/or the process around the reviews is cumbersome. This might be a testament to the bureaucracy that has seeped into today's corporate environment.

I wrote this book to help professional women succeed in corporate situations, especially those who feel powerless in a male-dominated corporate environment. I want to help.

First, let's get you women in the positions of power that you need to be in and then you can change these processes so that more professionals – both men and women – can all be empowered. There are men (and, I'm sure women) who have succumbed to just going down the line of employees to be reviewed, basically choosing a middle of the road score to make it look fair – possibly changing it up a bit here and there so it looks like they have given it more consideration than they actually have – not giving anyone too high of a score to raise any suspicion or that I am favoring anyone". These are true confessions that I have heard many times.

I was told by a male shareholder of a professional services firm, "I never give anyone a five." (A was the highest ranking in their review process.) I asked him why, of course. "I just don't." Curious, I prodded, "Would you give yourself a five?" "Maybe... I don't know." He replied. Relentless (as I am) I pushed, "Tell me more about your thought process on this." In the end, he changed his mind about not giving five. He realized that by discounting that ranking, he was actually completely changing the skew of the system, giving himself only four levels by which to rank someone.

I recall a time when I was asked to review my own performance (such a great practice I think) and I gave myself overall very high rankings. My reviewer raised an eyebrow and commented, "I notice you have given yourself a very high ranking across the board." I smiled slightly and nodded. He waited for me to say something. "I consider myself a very motivated, effective professional. I continue to educate myself to stay completely current on the issues that face the shareholders and this firm. I monitor my programs and budget as if it was my own money. I make sure that everyone is regularly aware of my activities and accomplishments and the value that I provide here. If there is ever a sense that I've fallen short in an area, I get myself back up to speed – I don't wait for review time. So I feel I have continued to demonstrate high marks in all the areas that I was asked to assess." For better or worse, after that conversation I was not reviewed for another five years. However, I continued to send regular accomplishment reports to him and other key shareholders on a regular basis. I'm not sure whether or not this was the reason I was not reviewed. I feel I should have been given the chance to review my own performance and hear from others; I think this is an important business practice. I will say that as long as I was employed in Corporate, I always made a point of communicating my value on a regular basis (being careful to use a tone that reflected the perspective of those who supervised me) and I always received top raises. How often you send out your own accomplishment report is up to you. I would suggest twice a month or monthly. And if it's ever time to update your resume, you'll have ample content.

Hint: a long bullet list of accomplishments that lists what you did, for whom and why (the desired result, preferably reflected in %, $ or #s) at a glance, will impress any boss or perspective employer.

Let's Talk About Money - Salary & Raises

What about salary negotiations? Empowered women are happy with the amount of money they make at work. What makes them happy about how much money they make? There are some very interesting differences between men and women. Over the years, I have read the most fascinating and enlightening statistics: 60% of men will apply for a job they feel they are not fully qualified for, while women only apply for jobs they feel completely (100%) qualified for. During salary negotiations, if a male job candidate throws out the first number – and it is accepted, a male will feel regret whereas, in the same, situation, a woman will feel relief. So many women struggle with this issue. It is good to understand our obstacles around money. Many of us have been told that even *talking* about money is distasteful. If we believe that money is the root of all evil and we feel alienated from the rich, it will continue to be hard to attract money to us. It is our culture to envy the rich (and famous, for that matter) in a very unhealthy way. After all, the only difference between rich people and not so rich people stems from their attitude about money. Rich people never feel guilty for having it, do they? And why should they? It is simply a neutral, isn't it? It's not money, per say, that means anything – it's what it gets us, right? I urge all women to re-think their deeply seated hidden biases around money. Accept it as your right. Receive! More, I say!

You have to really, truly believe that you're worth it before you tell the boss how much you want.

When women are talking to other women it's easier, I think, to offer

"Let's talk money via e-mail." I have often added, with a laugh, "I may negotiate my fee but I'll do so via e-mail because I'm braver that way." This way, I'm honestly telling the other person that this is my preference for negotiating my fee. I'm simply stating what I want. I want to negotiate money via e-mail because that's what I'm more comfortable with. Can you do that next time you're discussing your raise or a fee? Who would deny you this, with good reason? If you deliver this statement with sincerity I think it will work – it has always worked for me. I, too, do not like to discuss money. But, I also like to negotiate and win a big fee!

Some things to consider when you are an empowered woman at work and you have the power to offer jobs to others and negotiate their salaries:

- Assess what the job is worth, not the person.

- Don't ask about previous salary history because it's irrelevant.

- Don't give raises on what is going to be done (promises), give raises based on past performance.

- Be completely transparent about the process by which you are hiring or distributing pay increases and make it known, clearly. This goes for levels of promotions, too (i.e. "How do you get your own office at this place?" I was once asked). Who knew?

- Consider offering a compensation that rewards your professionals for living and breathing whatever core values you have adopted.

- Compensate on a number of areas of performance – traditional things like billable rate, sales quotas, etc.; non-traditional areas such as marketing or client satisfaction/service; and completely intangible qualities that are valued – such as honesty and compassion.

Hint: Incentive compensation programs can be customized to reward professionals who excel in certain key areas as well as the well-rounded professional – someone who is good at many things, but does not excel in one particular area of expertise. It takes all kinds to make a company work and we are God's special children!

Empowered women help each other to get ahead at work. Sadly, I see more support among women in a corporate environment after they're in their 40s. I believe it might be because of a number of different possibilities – perhaps the 20s are lost to some young women who are still trying to figure out what they want or who they are; the 30s might be lost for some women to childrearing and/or they might not be so quick to help other women their age during this time because of a sense of competition with their peers – and it could be a combination of all that and more. But whenever you are ready and able, please do select another woman to sponsor. I'm not talking about just mentoring here or giving another woman your ear over lunch once in a while. I'm strongly suggesting you find another woman at your company (no matter what age) and help her to achieve greatness at your place of employment. Go out of your way to let others know of her strengths and accomplishments, publicly sing her praises whenever you can and go out on a limb for her at least once. Consider who that might be at your work right now – and set a date for lunch. Go ahead. Do it!

Demonstrating your value means giving yourself what you need – in life and at work. Before you leave work each day, think about (or write down) one thing for which you have to grateful. Was someone kind to you today? Did someone give you something? Their time or attention? Did you feel that someone really heard you? These are all special gifts. Try to thank someone each and every day for something at work. Every day. Start today and make this a daily practice. Finally, make sure you are getting enough vacation time. I have not seen this to be a problem with women; however, I warn you to ensure you at least get some time for yourself. (Many women who have children schedule all their free time with their children's needs in mind). Family vacations, as we know, are not always – ever? – relaxing, so consider adding on one more day and go somewhere just by yourself – even if it's just a pedicure or a glass of wine with a friend.

10 - Empowered Women At Work...Stay Educated and Current in their Field

I remember when my brother found out that I was going to graduate school, the first thing he said was, "you like school don't you." The only thing I could do is laugh and say, "Yeah."

Shortly after obtaining a double master's in Practical Theology and Human Service counseling, I took a weekend life coach course. I had just been credentialed as a life coach a few months earlier but in my opinion, you just can't have enough education. Why am I so driven? I can't help but feel in order to give the best, I must *be* the best.

I remain educated in a significant and unforeseen way that demonstrates "over and above commitment" to my clients in a multiplicity of ways. I do this by continuously exposing myself to every educational opportunity I can think - or dream of – especially if it relates to achieving dreams, enhancing a feeling of self-worth or anything else that can improve an individual's life, especially during midlife. On a daily basis I am searching for courses to take, online or in person. If I am not searching for courses, I am listening to webinars weekly. In addition, to attending courses and listening to webinars, I continuously educate myself by becoming a member of professional organizations, which assist in learning about new products and industry trends.

One of the most rewarding ways I like to stay abreast of the coaching industry is networking. Networking not only assists in learning but it is an ideal way to brainstorm. However, the 21st century offers numerous ways for me to continue to remain educated through social media. Twitter is a great way to connect with industry leaders to learn more about life coaching and midlife. LinkedIn allows me to get the latest updates from related industries, groups and individuals. I am constantly on YouTube to learn about midlife and coaching techniques. In one way or another, free or paid, I seek ways to make myself a better life coach through education. This helps me to further assist my clients to find their life's purpose and move toward their destiny – despite them thinking their life is over because they have reached a certain age.

My strong commitment to education has not gone without obstacles. In addition to my passion for coaching, I maintain another career as a realtor and have family commitments that take precedence, at times. In addition, for better or worse, I have a "do-it-all" personality where I try to be a superwoman.

Nonetheless, I will continue to educate myself to "go over and above" and will always be committed to reinvention, rediscovery and reinvigoration – and I suggest you do the same!

- Patricia Dinkens – Strategic Midlife Transformational Coach
  Founder, SMT Coaching

In this day and age, the playing field for professional women is getting more competitive. If you are an empowered woman or want to be, this is not a bad thing. If you are changing things at work for yourself good for you! As part of the commitment to positive changes for yourself, you should be ready, willing and able to invest in yourself. You must stay educated. Current. "In the know." With the ease of technology, we have Google news alerts to find out about what our customers are up to (and our competitors), we have audio books, we can subscribe to trade-focused newsletters and broadcast e-mails (the good ones; the ones we don't want to delete) and we even have on-line degrees that are available at reasonable costs. There are books that can be immediately downloaded on digital devices and whitepapers – the list goes on and on. You must be educating and improving yourself regularly. Read one business book in between a few fiction books. Join one targeted organization for the purposes of educating yourself about a new service area or a different customer base. Look to join a mastermind group of some kind. Hand pick your network with other smart, thought-provocative people who can stretch your mind and shake your opinions about things – provide healthy debate or challenge the way you see things. Please don't be stagnant. Remember, if it's a subject you love, it's not boring. Depending upon what type of professional you are, there should be some way to bridge the gap between what you love and what you do. It might be tricky, but it usually can be done. Don't ever stop growing, keep learning and asking questions.

By the way, personally, one of the biggest leaps that I made, in terms of improvement in my professional abilities, was when I gave myself permission to stop all reactionary activity and allow myself to focus on one thing – for as long as it took. How do you think I wrote a book? (I shut down my outlook for long periods of time). No phone, no texts, nothing (well, a few stretches here and there).

Brain research shows that it's literally impossible to multi-task – to consider more than one thing at a time. Multi-tasking is the ability to manage the transfer of your attention more quickly between tasks. Women are often praised for their ability to multi-task. It might be that women are better able to multi-task – or "switch gears" - but I believe it has more to do with how women holistically ponder numerous aspects of the issues they are trying to solve.

It remains a challenge, nonetheless, to effectively problem-solve when trying to deal with more than one task at a time. It's impossible to do good work with constant distraction and interruption – yet that is exactly how we have set up most work environments, haven't we?

With knowledge comes responsibility. Now that you know your people can't concentrate the way things are, what are you going to do about it? If you can't change how others work, then start showing them how it's done by example. It's one thing to close your door for the morning or work from home, but quite another to make sure that the powers-that-be understand the value of your having done so.

Bob: "Where were you this morning?" Julie: "I was finally able to complete that report for the client," Julie reports with a big smile. "I took care of it offsite since it would have taken two-three days if I was here in the office, because of all the distraction." Bob is impressed (and jealous).

11 - Empowered Women At Work...Improve Their Environment to Better Suit Them

I was born and raised in LA. At the age of 29 I found myself living at home, working a job I did not understand and actually hated. I was a human resources benefit administrator and I lost more sleep working that job then I ever want to lose again. I was not financially stable and had a constant fear of getting fired. That nightmare became a reality when I was let go from the job. I felt like a total failure and could not shake the feeling. On paper people were impressed with my degrees (BA in journalism an MPP in public policy) but on the inside I could not understand why others were impressed with me. I knew I should be impressed with myself, despite what others think, but that was not the case.

I had visited Washington DC but I did not really get to experience the city until my internship in 2012. I fell in love with the city and knew I wanted to live there someday. It was full of young people that were determined to change the world for the better. I remembered how people talked about politics and their desire to create better public policies. I was slightly turned off by how competitive the city appeared, but overall I really liked DC.

Back in Los Angeles I was constantly surrounded by people who wanted to be in the entertainment business particularly producing, directing, modeling, acting, singing and dancing. It seemed superficial. To be honest, I was overweight, dissatisfied with my physical appearance and generally annoyed with my life in Los Angeles.

In January of 2014, I sold my car and packed my life into 3 large suitcases and moved to DC. I couldn't afford to move to DC so my faithful mother came with me to help me get settled. I registered with a temp agency and immediately began working on various short-term assignments. This move forced me to get to know myself like never before.

It was winter in DC and for a southern California girl anything below 60 degrees is freezing. I was pretty upset with the weather but happy to have my own place. I relied on my faith in ways I did not know humanly possible.

The ensuing year was great because it forced me out of my comfort zone. I was living on my own in a city of my choice and surrounded myself with things that I valued. I was also forced to take public transportation everywhere and live by a budget – among other things that I had not done in LA. Overall, my journey is helping me to harness my desires and eradicate my fears in order to live the abundant life I was called to live.

- Teri A. – Event Planner, Washington D.C.

Women are much more affected by their physical environment than men. I have seen so many problems arise in the workplace because no one has stopped to plan the flow of the work space appropriately. No one usually gives this any attention and, when they do - if it's a man - he will approach this very differently than a woman.

Earlier in my career, I worked for a man who was the head of a large department of over 40 employees. He was to oversee the move of this accounting department from one location to another. Everyone was excited because they had been promised they were all going to get new workstations. I accompanied the male department on a tour some top-notch office furniture at a large showroom in Long Island, New York. The furniture was beautiful. Before I left for the tour of the available office furniture, I took the liberty of touring the current department, interviewing our employees about their current workstations – what was working well and what wasn't, what they needed, what they would love, etc. I made lots of notes and was well-equipped to make my recommendation at the end of the tour. After selecting a beautiful line of furniture that would work out very well, we were left with choices between three levels of workstations – say, A, B and C. A was the smallest workstation design and, as such, was the most affordable. Conversely, B was middle of the road while the C workstation was the largest and the "top of the line" for that line of furniture. I suggested that we choose the middle tier of workstation based on the interviews I conducted. The B station had enough overhead storage, taller divisions for privacy and enough room for a personal drawer for each employee. At the last minute, after calculating the numbers, the male department head decided that it would be cheaper to go with A, and so, based on that pure fact alone, despite my best attempts to change his mind, that is what everyone got. Two years later I visited the department and was appalled at what I saw! There were stacks of papers and boxes around everyone's stations, literally spilling out into the floor. There was no privacy for anyone because the walls were so low and personal items – like coats and handbags were thrown all about the place. The energy in that place was oppressive and after greeting the people I quickly realized that morale was at an all-time low. I asked the man in charge about it. "How's it working out?" He said it was fine.

Women have a different aesthetic than men – have you noticed? The bachelor pad is often deemed as such because of the lack of attention to fashion rather than function. This is why you will see a man just drape over a long extension cord for a plug that dangles entirely across the garage. A wife may notice this with frustration because it has a negative impact on her (not all women, but most). Just like the woman who feels compelled to pick up a sock while a man doesn't notice it all. Physical space matters to women. I ask my female clients about their physical space at work all the time. Although some women don't have the same need for warmth in their environment in order to feel comfortable, most are greatly affected by their physical – and many are not aware how much so. They don't decorate their office because the men don't. But this can have a very positive impact on morale and productivity. Colors, lighting and placement of furniture greatly affects not only movement within the space, often streamlining productivity but it also impacts mood, appetite and work ethic. Things like temperature, natural sunlight (vs. fluorescent lighting) can have a tremendous impact. A lack of a door to close or a quiet place to access can be bothersome (how do you call your gynecologist to get your pap test results over the phone with no privacy?)

I realize that not everyone in a corporate environment gets their own office. I know that workstations have been designed to create a feeling of warm, personal space with dividers between spaces for private conversations. Partitions can be used in a very creative way to provide the illusion of privacy and more space. I have seen it work beautifully, efficiently and cost-effectively. I have seen great examples of how women positively affect the physical work environment – such as bringing in pillows, shutting off the overhead fluorescent lighting and bringing in table lamps, listening to soft music in the background, using a decorative space heater, personal artwork, aromatherapy and even water features.

I have witnessed so many dehumanizing incidents at work because of a lack of considerate planning in office environment as I've been on the receiving end of a tour being given to me by a man, who is proudly showing me the new office space.   Open space environments where everyone is jam-packed into a large open room and, at least in two specific incidents, I was told that personal belongings must be out of clear sight – so, no family photos or other personal reminders. There are no couches in many corporate environments in the U.S. (In Asian countries this is common, and naps are also encouraged, by the way.) And, although one of the reasons is the long work hours, another reason is that if you're tired you should be able to take a nap – human beings get tired.

Once, when I was in my 20s, having just started a new job only a few weeks earlier, I fainted on the elevator. I was dragged over to a wall where I sat up against it waiting for help. I very much wanted to lie down but there was no couch anywhere. It was quite uncomfortable and embarrassing. At a minimum, I think a work environment should have a couch somewhere in case someone really needs to lie down.

What about the lack of a private space in the work environment for nursing mothers? Or sick employees? Just as you must have regular fire drills, you should allow for the fact that human beings get sick – at some point, we will appreciate a place to be quiet, to rest, even to sleep at work. As an empowered woman, you should bring these issues up to the powers-that-be. Here's what I suggest:

When you go into work tomorrow, look around at the space. As you walk through different areas, picture how it would be if you were assigned to that space. Pay attention to things like smell and temperature and the mood you pick up on as you pass through the various departments. I have visited offices that keep the temperature so cold that it was hard for me to type because, although I was wearing a sweater, my fingers were stiff from the cold.

Think about how visitors are impacted by the reception area. Smell the space as you walk through. How is the air quality? (I am very sensitive to smells and can tell you that I have smelled mold in many offices that I have visited).

Above & Beyond Perks in the Work Environment

I have heard complaints about company-wide illness that correlates to construction on a floor above or below. I have worked for companies that regularly tested the air quality of the office space to ensure that it was a healthy work environment.

I have enjoyed taking – and giving – exercise classes for corporations who value having gyms in their offices. In many cases, there are contests and parties and charitable fundraisers connected with the endeavor – such as company-sponsored bike rides or marathons. One company ran fun, athletic games on bring your child to work day. This is a fabulous way to encourage healthy living for staff. Currently, I have spent the last 15 years providing lunch time spinning classes for an insurance company. This company has a full gym in their building and encourages their professionals to exercise during lunch (and gives them 90 minutes each day to do so). The company reports that the program has boosted morale and greatly reduced illness and call outs. (It also keeps their employees – and me - in shape!) Can you squeeze in exercise during your work day – and get paid for it?

Is any of this the responsibility of the empowered woman?

I believe that empowered women are more aware of these things and are willing to bring such issues to the attention of the powers-that-be (i.e. office manager or owner of the building) so that the work environment supports the company and what it does in all ways possible. A comfortable, healthy safe work force is a more productive one and a pleasant one.

Because we spend so much time at work, I think we should enjoy our physical space there whenever possible. This goes for our own workspace, whether it be private or not – and common areas, such as the reception area and the lunchroom / kitchen. Because I have always been so keenly affected by my own surroundings and am obsessed with interior design – and because I have observed such differences in mood, morale and productivity after witnessing so many changes that my female clients have made to their environment (both at home and work) as a result of our conversations – I will happily share with you some of the most beneficial and easy changes that you can make next week in your office – please do empower yourself to pick at least one or two that you can apply right away to positively impact your work space.

Lighting – I am very averse myself to fluorescent lighting. Many women are, as well, I have found. It is also very unflattering and maddening when one of the bulbs gets low and starts to flutter. Consider bringing in a lamp set to use if you have a private office. I have found that one stand up lamp and one table top or desk lamp is more than enough to provide you with enough lighting and improve the mood in your office. Most of the women who make this change report that their office visitors stay longer and seem much more relaxed. If you have a workstation in a general or common space, a table lamp or desk lamp to use for surface work can greatly reduce eye strain as well as be calming.

Furniture placement – The placement of your furniture – in your office or throughout common work spaces – can greatly impact the flow of the work being done. It might be as simple as re-evaluating how your space works (think of the kitchen triangle that most designers discuss: take food out of fridge, place it by sink for cleaning, and then place it in the oven. Another example is that the dishwasher be near the sink as well as the cabinet or shelf where the dishes are to be stored. This way you are minimizing your energy while you complete regular tasks. Can you apply this concept to your workplace? Are things where they should be, making your flow easy? Thinking bigger about workflow can also greatly assist productivity at work. I have had many discussions about how best to arrange professionals in the work environment – by service area, by the type of client serviced (or niche area) and by other criteria. As always, since there is a pro and con to every scenario, these are choices that will have to be made. I suggest that groups or teams work best in terms of placement. Groups share something in common and teams share the same goals around accomplishment. So a group can be sorted by title, designation, knowledge (service area) and a team is a group of individuals that share the same goal – i.e. sales teams, client service teams, industry teams can also be an effective way of sorting people out best. Another great idea is to ask your staff how they feel it would work best. As I write, this I have a professional client who has been so negatively impacted by the physical department she has been assigned to that she is negotiating a transfer to another section on the other side of the building. She will also transfer some of her duties to adjust to this move. The rapport, work flow, demands and management style of the old department all have contributed to this decision – and, thankfully, for her, her suggestion to be moved (and why) was well-received by the powers-that-be to make it happen for her. She is an empowered woman!

Temperature – If the temperature in your office or work environment is not right, try to fix it. If you can't fix it for everyone, then take the brave step of attempting to fix it for yourself – and watch others take notice. If it's hot, bring in a fan; if it's cold, bring in a space heater. If people have comments about it, use the opportunity to create a dialogue around creating an impetus for improvement and/or solution to the problem.

Ergonomics – Ergonomics addresses attention to posture and comfort while working. This topic is so very important. I have seen disastrous work environments and when it comes to ergonomics, the most common issue falls to seating. Many professionals just take whatever seat they're given without a care as to their posture. In fact, most people who do have a good chair might still not pay proper attention to the adjustment of its height, or slope, or any other fancy adjustments that might be available. The lumbar region is the lower back and this is the most common area for back pain, when seating properly isn't addressed. A lumbar pillow can usually work wonders and you can pick one from any store at a very reasonable price (it can also help your office space look more attractive). Your keyboard should be an appropriate distance from your torso and your fingers should fall over it with a slight bend (think of playing a piano). I often cringe when I see professionals slumped over a lap top on a desk surface that is too high for comfortable typing.

The neck and upper back often can be strained at work. I have found this to be the most critical area for me as it is the area where I hold the most stress. Back in the day, I will admit to feeling slightly intimidated about using a headset. Then I got one myself – WOW! Not only is it great because you will no longer hold a telephone receiver in the crook of your neck, but many of the headsets available now can be used directly with your PC, making you sound impeccable when conducting webinars or listening to videos in silence among co-workers. Everything sounds crystal clear. Don't let anyone else's comments in the office keep you from achieving maximum comfort during work hours.

Breaks / Exercise – It is recommended that you get up and walk or move around every 90 minutes. This is also how often your brain switches hemispheric dominance (changing from a more linear, analytical approach to processing information to a more holistic, imagination focused approach – or vice versa). It's very beneficial to get up and move – even to find a place to stretch – or have something to drink or a small snack.

Natural Light – As above, if you can take 10 minutes or so for a walk outside to make sure some natural light gets on your face, do so. I always say a breeze on your cheek is like a gentle kiss from God (or heaven, or your happy place) and even if it's cold, being out in nature is good for you. If you can, try to slip your shoes off and feel the ground or grass under your feet. It's called "earthing" and it can help you to feel more grounded. Try this when you have a difficult conversation waiting or if you're upset about something. Another thing you might do is give yourself some meditative time.

Privacy / Rejuvenation – If you have a private office, please do consider shutting your door at least once a day for some re-energizing. I've had some professionals tells me they use their headset to watch a shot meditation video on YouTube or just sit quietly in meditation. Some listen to a visualization. Some call their friend or child behind closed doors so they can speak freely. Some get up, kick their shoes off and do a full body short stretching routine (this is what I used to do – regularly. It made all the difference in the world.) If you don't have an office, use the time on that short, outside walk to quietly focus on a thing in nature and try to let all your thoughts go… let them pass like a cloud. Meditation during the workday – even for five to ten minutes – can quiet your mind, clear the cobwebs of hidden bias and limiting beliefs and provide answers to long-standing problems. They can provide the "Aha!" moments that can change your day – or even your life – at work.

Energy Preservation – People who remain "on" and available to others throughout the entire day for long hours without a break can suffer from it – and it often shows. Weight gain, fatigue, disgruntlement, lack of focus, etc. is often a result of being worn down. Find something that will rejuvenate you. I have seen some professionals bounce back from playing a computer game, reading a book at lunch, or going out to a lunch with a friend - anything to break up the monotony of the office environment – and reduce the stress from being "on" all day.

I had no idea how draining life in a Monday through Friday, 9:00 am to 5:00 pm corporate environment was until I left it. I had no idea how much energy I depleted each and every day. From bouncing up to an alarm to jump in a shower, dressing up in business attire, driving or taking public transportation (both of which presented enormous stresses) and then greeting my co-workers with that "Good Morning" smile, I was giving it my all for a minimum of 10 hours each and every day – and for so many years without any kind of real break. Now I manage my time and energy much better and have been able to be more productive and content as a result.

Noise reduction/privacy – The hums of machinery, the noises of colleagues, or the annoyance of announcements over an intercom or piped in music can all offer unrest and disruptions that most will come to overlook. But these noises can prove to usurp your concentration and energy – and affect your mood. It can be tricky to avoid but some of my empowered women professionals have used tricks such as noise machines (to play either white noise or particular sounds, like the rainforest or the ocean) or radios turned down low.

Remember that if you are working remotely, you will want to address all this from your remote work space as well. The same things that might distract and annoy you at work can do the same at home. A final note on this, too, is that if you look around your home and can find no special place of peace or solace that is just yours, it might be time to create one. A special place of beauty and calm is necessary – both at work and at home – for any empowered woman. A soft chair, a beautiful painting or image, a scented candle that reminds you of someplace happy, a pillow that you look at across the room… these are things that an add a bit of beauty and peace to you throughout each day.

12 - Empowered Women At Work...Acknowledge Family Dynamics

When I was young and in the Navy, I honestly never experienced gender issues like I did when I entered into corporate America.

I chose the field of healthcare systems and it was my job to oversee collections and revenue cycles. I quickly realized that I had a lot to learn. I felt like I had to work harder and so I put in longer hours. Back then, my work came first, despite trying to balance a family. I was stressed all the time. It was never enough.

And then it dawned on me one day, during a meeting where the managers (that meant me) were being pushed hard to meet a very tight deadline to convert all our paper documents to digital. The deadline was August 1st. "This could really ruin my summer," I thought. As I listened to management putting on the pressure, I realized something. No matter how we tracked the financial information, the numbers would stay the same. Further, when pressed, they admitted that they would buffer the conversion by using both systems for quite some time. I decided to give myself a break.

I thought to myself, "The numbers concerning the revenue collections will always add up. What doesn't add up is putting my kids second."

I realigned, in that moment, and decided to change my outlook then and there. My kids would come first from now on. At 38-years-old, I started owning that I *did* know what I was doing and that, whether I worked five hours or 20 hours, the numbers would speak for themselves. I stepped into the fact that I'm a professional person – I know as much, or more, than other people I am working with. I fully understand that work is important but when you have children, it is not the most important thing.

That was my moment and I put my foot down during that meeting. I told them I would try to have all my departments converted on time but that I planned on doing it more right than fast. I told them that I would not be staying late or working during weekends and advised my salaried staff to do the same.

That was the day I stopped asking for permission and started stating "….this is how I'm going to do it."

I enjoyed 10 more years of being respected at that company.

- Rebeca Watkins – Director of Business & Revenue Cycle, United Health Services, Former Director of Operations, Tenet Health Systems, Former Corpsman Second Class, United States Navy

I once was washing my hands in a women's restroom when I heard the familiar sound of a small motor – a breast pump. I figured there was a woman in a stall, sitting on a toilet, pumping breast milk. This infuriated me. It really did. As a manager, I had my own office but this poor woman clearly did not. Of course, I found her afterwards and spoke to her in private. Many larger, corporate environments today do have a private room or even a pumping room, although one I saw made me cringe. But most office environments do not provide such a private space; however, women should feel empowered enough to ask for one. I was easily able to arrange for this woman to use a spare office and she was grateful.

Motherhood - Depending upon how you view it - can either empower you at work or undermine you. It's your choice. Why do I say that? Because perception is reality. That's really what this whole book is about. Believe it to be true – and it is. Simple? In concept, yes it is. In practical application? Very hard. Allow me to examine my own theory in more detail. When I became pregnant at the age of 38, I was working for a professional services firm, serving in the role of director of marketing. I was established there and had my own office. I was the only marketing person at this firm and, as such, performed my duties rather autonomously, basically running my own show as it were. I resisted telling anyone I was pregnant for as long as I could. Why?

Because, to be honest, I knew that it would change how I was perceived. I knew I would get asked lot of personal questions. My least favorite of which was, "Was it planned?" I have always thought to be a very rude question, but politely tolerated it because of my advanced age. My response was a truthful one. "Yes, we decided to try to have a baby and I, thankfully, got pregnant right away."

Looking back, holding off telling people I was pregnant spared me months of some really stupid conversations. And if you have even been pregnant at work, you know what I mean. Hopefully, you don't. But probably you do. And, of course, the most annoying conversations started with one stupid question.

"Will you be coming back to work?" Arrrrgggghhhhh! Really? For men, this isn't even an option. And for most women, it isn't an option either. Statistics report that only 19% of American families are made up of one male bread-winner and one female home-maker. Once when I was about to facilitate a webinar for a group of HR professionals, I overheard the chair of the committee (of human resources professionals and firm administrators) ask the organizer of the event, who was pregnant at the time, if she would be coming back to work. This was before the recording started, thank goodness, but there were many folks already on the call. Most of them were women and I know they overheard this. The woman replied that yes, she would be coming back to work after a maternity leave. Note: I am not going to get into this but PLEASE! Do not vote for an elected official that does not support paid maternity leave in your state. At the time of my pregnancy, living in Pennsylvania, maternity leave was not a state-wide mandate. Paid leave could only be covered by short disability which my firm did not offer. I saved up my money so I could stay home for six weeks – unpaid. And, of course, unless you are living under a rock, you will know that in many countries around the world, women get a full year of paid leave from work to stay home and care for babies. A male colleague of mine recently told me that he sat in on an interview process to select a judge in his state. One of the candidates was a woman with six children and she was asked

how she would manage the job considering the demands of her large family. She responded politely, explaining that she had a strong support system from extended family members and her husband, etc. My friend cringed at this question and said, "A man would never be asked that." I'm shaking my head as I write this.

Empowered women realize there is a delicate balance of mixing personal and professional. How much sharing about family is appropriate? Which topics are more permissible to share and what might stir objection? My experience offers some guidelines.

I commented to a vendor I was dealing with that I had been waiting for her to return my call, as it had been three days since I asked for her expected deliverable. She excused herself by explaining, "Well, you know school just started and I've been so busy getting the kids ready." I was miffed. If you are using your family demands as an excuse or reason for not meeting a deadline or providing a deliverable, you are most likely alienating a boss or client. In certain, severe situations, such as with a chronically ill family member that requires frequent hospitalization or abundant care, this may obviously become unavoidable. However, I am talking about the normal demands of family life that should not affect the workplace.

A female professional relayed that a male co-worker was giving her a hard time at work. She felt that he didn't respect her. I encouraged her to have an honest conversation with him. She was able to ascertain that he felt she was "talking too much about her family". Specifically, he was under the impression that she was unwilling to go above and beyond for the clients they served. He told her he felt this way because she was very vocal about how she planned her work schedule around her family time. He heard her complain about her workload as it was negatively impacting her time with her young daughter.

She was able to convince him of her commitment to her work and her ability to serve clients, going "above and beyond." She explained an incident where she had to refuse to take a call from home after hours because she would have been home alone with her child and was afraid that she would make too much noise in the background. (If you have been the mother of a toddler, you know that young children always fuss when you pick up a phone). She began to honestly assess how she said things and how often she mentioned her family. She grew to realize how some of her comments about her family could be construed as a lack of enthusiasm for her work. As always, there are two sides to this coin. The empowered woman remains aware of how much she talks about her family in the workplace. Sharing family issues and joys with co-workers and customers can foster rapport but too much talk about family and children's accomplishments can alienate others. Reading cues from others should help gauge when it's time to stop talking about your family and stay focused on work. Just as you would be careful as to how long you spend on a personal call while in the office, be aware of how much to discuss your personal life at work.

Most professionals – male and female – will excuse themselves to take a call from a child during the workday. I remember hearing the receptionist announce that the school nurse was calling for one of my co-workers who had an office next to me. She was in a meeting down the hall. I did not hesitate to interrupt that meeting to alert her to take the call. No one minded.

The truth is that children more often call mothers over their fathers. Although children need to be taught not to call too often or for no good reason (such as settling arguments with siblings) sometimes a child does need to talk to his or her parent. Don't be ashamed to take calls from family members if they need you – and don't make excuses for it. However, do excuse yourself - in the form of taking those calls privately. The empowered woman takes all personal calls with family members in private.

If you are working when you become a mother or are working with someone who has, please show your support. It should not be looked down upon to leave work early to pick up a sick child from school. Thankfully, more and more 30-something dads are proudly announcing that they are leaving to attend the soccer practice – and less people are flinching. This is a good trend and one that must continue to be supported. Flex time is going to be critical to continuing to do work in the arena of professional services. Between the convenience of technology as well as some enlightened minds, and remote access becoming more widely adopted in the workplace, moms and dads can go home and have dinner with their families and then get back online and finish their work in the evening. We must support this allocation of work-life fit or else we are bound to have a de-energized, disempowered and flailing workforce – not to mention the ill effects of the generation of children behind these disillusioned parents. I could tell you so many horror stories here. But I'll just share a few of the secrets of the female professionals I have worked with (using different names, of course).

13 - Empowered Women At Work...Share Their Secrets with Other Women

It was a few years ago and my firm was combining with another large accounting firm. What I now refer to as my *"Lean In"* moment came just days after finishing the book of the same name, which had left me feeling brave and inspired.

I was the manager of our firm's women's initiative (WomenCAN at CohnReznick). I had a clear vision of where I wanted to take things and believed I was the most knowledgeable about what needed to change. The combination of cultures could be a challenge, I realized, and some of the prior conversations about the WomenCAN initiative had me feeling doubtful.

I was walking down the hall, headed to a pivotal strategy meeting with the new Steering Committee – four of the most influential women leaders from the legacy firms. I was excited to bring together, face to face, these women who would now strongly influence this national company's diversity strategy and I had allotted three hours for a meaningful collaboration. I had a lot vested in this.

As I turned a corner, I literally bumped into our CEO.

Given my role as a coach and a career advocate for women, I think it's very important to walk the walk, as well as talk the talk. So, when I saw the opportunity, I knew I had to take it. I walked over to him told him about our planned meeting. I said, "If you have 15 minutes, please stop by." And, to my pleasant surprise, he did.

We were discussing how we would need to spearhead our approach as an organizational culture change. I was pitching more than a program. I wanted to create a strategy that would begin to address subconscious bias and reveal hidden barriers that interfered with our ability to keep women in the pipeline and on the partner track. I explained that diversity should be a priority and that it will take buy-in from the top.

I turned to my CEO and asked, "What's your buy-in? How committed are you to this?"

He answered, "Women represent half of this firm. If you need dollars, I have them. If you need resources, I have them, too." *Thank you Tom Marino!* I can't tell you how empowered I felt at that moment – I had taken a chance that day and it paid off - big time. I now felt completely confident to proceed with my original plan. I rapidly shared this success story with my local office liaison team which has now grown into 50 representatives in more than 20 offices across the U.S.

My secret: Put yourself out there, take a risk and see what happens. *Pass it on!*

   - Michelle Lifschitz – Manager, Women CAN: the Collaborative Advocacy Network at CohnReznick

Kimberly, a top-notch member of the management team at her place of employment, only leaves at 5:00 pm if she carries her laptop and a huge file of papers with her out the door. She even takes the long route out of the office so she is seen by her colleagues. She admits to me that she does this often. I ask her, "Do you ever work on any of it?" "Never", she replies. "I bet your back hurts", I say. She laughs, "It's heavy!" I ask her, "Do other males in your office ever leave at 5:00 – ever?" She admits that surely, they do – and when they do they are more likely to just walk out the door with a wave and a wink. I ask her, "Do you think you can give yourself permission to do the same?" "Starting tomorrow, I will try that." Whew.

Carol is also a senior professional with more than 30 years of experience and at the top in her field at work. She carries with her a tremendous amount of guilt over the amount of time she has spent at work. She admitted to me that she felt she was over-compensating by unnecessarily rewarding her children with extravagant gifts. She regretted the unrealistic expectations they developed as they had come to expect lavish gifts from her when she returned from business trips and complained that they know "just how to press my buttons" to make her feel guilty when they want something. Carol had to come to terms with the fact that she and her husband chose a different parental situation (he was the care-giver while she chose to pursue her career) and, with my encouragement, came clean with her kids about their expectations – as well as her guilt. When she asked her nine-year-old if she felt her mom had ever missed anything important in her life or neglected her, the child said no and Carol exhaled a deep sigh of relief. She forgave herself for her decision to work and could now carry on, guilt-free.

Pat is a CPA who is forced to work 10 to 12 hour workdays during tax season, including weekends. She cries to me that she hasn't seen her baby awake in nearly three weeks. At her firm, there is a rule. All professionals who are at a client site (this is common practice for CPA firms) must stay and work onsite – in pairs – until after dinner. The firm allows dinner to be expensed if they stay until a certain time of night (say, 7:00 or 7:30 pm). This means that Pat cannot get home in time to play with her baby. Pat would like to have this policy re-visited. She knows that she can do the work from home remotely.

I started to witness a shift in this thinking about the work-life dynamic from a male Baby Boomer just a few years ago. He started to share with me the many obstacles his own daughter was facing. I kept nodding sympathetically as he told me of her woes around maternity leave and juggling work-life balance. I waited for the right time to interject that other females around the office – including myself, were dealing with similar issues. This male, by the way, was head of HR at the firm. As I relayed his complaints to myself and his co-workers, I could see the light start to go off. When I pushed it though, he shut down. I could see his face change while he started to voice his resistance to approaching his other male Baby Boomer counterparts. "This place isn't ready for that much change, yet." So then he took the role of fellow complainer, not a doer. He chose to not take the issue up. After all, it wouldn't help his daughter. We need to start fighting the battles that will benefit us all, not just ourselves. Battles that will pave the way for our sons and our daughters.

Another glimmer of hope comes from Baby Boomers who are now faced with dealing with taking care of their aging parents. Finally, these males are coming to terms with dealing with the burden of caring for external family members. Circumstances seem to be forcing the males in this age group to pay attention to the details around care-giving for their elders and I am hopeful that this will arise in them more sympathy for women, who have traditionally taken on this role.

One more thing I wanted to add about the woman business-owner who often worked as a night owl. One of the things she admitted to me during our work together was that she often held off on sending e-mails that she drafted "in the middle of the night" because she was uncomfortable sending out messages with such a late time stamp. She would either take the time to save them in draft format and send them out the next afternoon or set them on a delay to go out in the morning. This took extra time and effort. I prodded her. She told me that one of the friends she had made recently, who turned out to be a great referral source, had caught her attention because she received a message from him very late one night. She was up and replied immediately and they had instant rapport over their unorthodox work hours. They bonded over this. I reminded her that there could be more like-minded people out there and encouraged her to take pride in the fact that she has designed a professional experience that works for her.

When I get up in the middle of the night and can't get back to sleep, it's usually because something is on my mind. I get up and address it immediately, and if it means sending an e-mail, I do so. This allows me to go back to sleep. I have had someone comment on a time stamp from one of my e-mails. I simply said, "Yes, I was up so I did a little work." I could add that it's better than lying there trying to get back to sleep. But I don't say that part. I say, "I am productive." And that is that. Smile.

Honoring Our Connection with All

The human race – happily or unhappily as it may be – is connected to each other. In professional circumstances, we are more likely to thrive with the help of others. We cannot, nor should we want to, do it alone. In order to be successful in business, community and/or family, we must learn to work together as a team. We need to acknowledge our strengths and solicit those who can help us to improve our efforts in areas where we are not as strong. This is how the world works best. I strongly advise you to consider who at your workplace can stand up for you and assist you in making the necessary strides so that you can be supported to moving to that next level of service – whatever that may mean for you personally and professionally. Once you have figured out what you want, in the long-term and in the short-term, find someone who can help you get over that next hurdle. Everyone who I have ever met, honestly, every successful woman who I have asked – fondly recalls the value received from their sponsors. I use that word specifically. Notice I did not use the word mentor. Mentors are fantastic at helping us figure out what we want – and don't want – from our professional lives. But a sponsor will get us to that next level. Get yourself a sponsor. Find someone that you can sponsor as well.

Honor your connection to everyone in your workplace. This means the receptionist, the custodian, the entry-level clerk. You'd be surprised at how many hidden sources there are for encouragement, loyalty and respect in your corporate environment. There is great energy to be obtained from showing kindness and being mindful at work. Empower all at every level to be the best they can be and you will reap the benefits of this.

Honor what you do, for whom you do it and the benefits it provides to the human race and/or our planet. If you work for a company that is less than conscientious about preserving our earth, consider how you might contribute to a better or healthier outcome. Consider spearheading initiatives at your place of employment that can foster a healthier environment.

I will continue to optimistically contemplate the future of an increasingly expanding and changing global environment, confident that the women of the world will continue to discover and harness their true power and greatly influence the future of our world in a positive way. I expect us all to be pleasantly surprised at the changes the world will see over the next 50 years. I hope I live long enough to enjoy them all! I trust that my daughter will and hope she will somehow be a part of it.

www.ingramcontent.com/pod-product-compliance
Lightning Source LLC
Chambersburg PA
CBHW071149200326
41519CB00018B/5173